# *Creative*
# PATCHWORK

## *with*
## *Appliqué and Quilting*

CONSULTANT EDITOR
Louise Bugeni

The Australian Women's Weekly craft library

# Contents

## QUILTS *for the* Bedroom

## QUILTS *for* Hanging

## MINIS *and* Lap Quilts

## FOR *home* Decorating

## SOME *quilting* Accessories

## GENERAL INSTRUCTIONS

### MEASUREMENTS

*Throughout the book we have provided both imperial and metric measurements. Fabric quantities are provided in metric first, with imperial conversions rounded out. The cutting instructions are provided in inches first, with conversions to centimetres given as accurately as possible. For each project, it is most important that you work in one form of measurement only; do not switch between measurements.*

Double Irish Chain Quilt

# QUILTS
## *for the*
# Bedroom

*Most quilters dream of making a*

*traditional large-scale quilt, to see a*

*time-honoured design writ large.*

*The quilts on the following pages*

*won't disappoint — the Double Irish*

*Chain, Dresden Plate and Lemoyne*

*Star are all based on classic patterns,*

*while the antique quilt will enable you*

*to recreate your own piece of history.*

*All involve more than a weekend's work,*

*but what quiltmaker would begrudge*

*time so well and pleasurably spent?*

*The use of sombre colours accented by surprisingly vibrant contrasts is typical of the Amish style ...*

# Lemoyne Star Quilt

*The lifestyle of the Amish people of North America is based upon simplicity, with their quilts being one of the most powerful expressions of that ideal. The use of sombre colours accented by surprisingly vibrant contrasts is typical of their unique style, and this Amish-inspired quilt, featuring the Lemoyne Star pattern, pays homage to this idea. It was not unusual for Amish women to work more than 20 stitches to the inch in their hand quilting, but don't despair! This quilting design still looks good if you can manage only five or six stitches to the inch.*

## MEASUREMENTS

Finished quilt measures approximately 178cm x 216cm (70" x 85").

## MATERIALS

- 0.2m x 115cm ($^1$/$_4$yd x 45") each of 12 assorted plain mustard, orange, red and brown fabrics, for pieced blocks and inner borders

- 0.2m x 115cm ($^1$/$_4$yd x 45") each of six assorted plain blue and plain purple fabrics, for pieced blocks

- 7.6m x 115cm ($8^1$/$_2$yds x 45") black fabric, for setting blocks and triangles, outer border and backing

- 0.4m x 115cm ($^1$/$_2$yd x 45") blue fabric, for binding

- 185cm x 225cm (73" x 89") cotton batting

- Coordinating machine thread

- Quilting thread

- Quilting needles (betweens)

- Template plastic or cardboard

## TEMPLATE

Trace outline of diamond printed on this page onto plastic or cardboard, referring to "Making Templates" on page 114. $^1/_4$" (6mm) seam allowance is **included** on template and in all given measurements.

## SEWING

### Lemoyne Star Blocks

The Lemoyne Star block consists of four Y-seam units, each unit containing three intersecting seams. Y-seam construction (**Diagrams 1–6**) leaves seam allowances free, giving a flat intersection. It is important to back-stitch at seam allowance dots, but not necessary to back-stitch at outside edges, as this stitching will be crossed and held by another seam.

From the 12 assorted fabrics, cut 80 corner squares, each $3^1/_2$" (8.8cm), and 20 squares, each $5^1/_2$" (14cm). Cut each $5^1/_2$" square diagonally twice, to give 80 right-angle triangles.

From black fabric, cut eight strips, each $2^5/_8$" (6.6cm) wide, across width of fabric, for central diamonds.

From the assorted plain blue/purple fabrics, cut eight strips, each $2^5/_8$" (6.6cm) wide, across width of fabric, for central diamonds.

Trace around diamond template on wrong side of each strip of black and blue/purple fabric; you will need 80 black and 80 blue/purple diamonds in all. Cut out diamonds.

**Y-seam units:** On wrong side of fabric, use a dot to mark $^1/_4$" (6mm) seam allowances in every corner of each blue/purple diamond, in one corner of each square and in the right-angle corner of each triangle (**Diagram 1**).

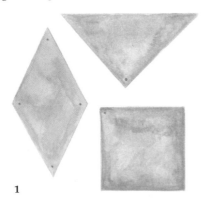

1

With right sides together and blue/purple diamond on top, stitch blue/purple diamond to black diamond along one edge, back-stitching at seam allowance dots (**Diagram 2**).

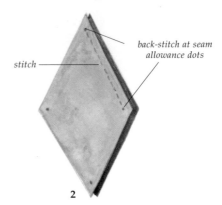

*stitch*

*back-stitch at seam allowance dots*

2

Open out triangles. With right sides together, pin blue/purple diamond to right-angle triangle so that dot on triangle corresponds exactly with top of seam on diamonds. Back-stitch at triangle dot and continue stitching to raw edge (**Diagram 3**).

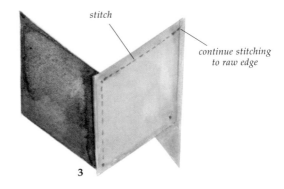

*stitch*

*continue stitching to raw edge*

3

Turn over and turn around the two diamonds and triangle so that the triangle is on top and the right angle is to the left (**Diagram 4**).

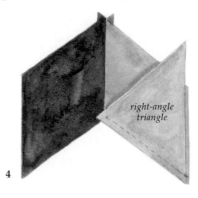

*right-angle triangle*

4

Swing triangle to edge of black diamond. With raw edges even, back-stitch at right-angle corner dot, then stitch to raw edge (**Diagram 5**).

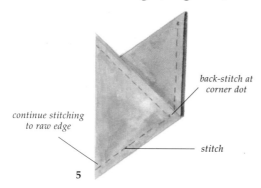

*continue stitching to raw edge*

*back-stitch at corner dot*

*stitch*

5

Press first seam allowance towards black diamond, then press triangle seam allowances towards diamonds, to complete the Y-seam unit (**Diagram 6**). For each block, make four of these units. (You will need 80 Y-seam units altogether.)

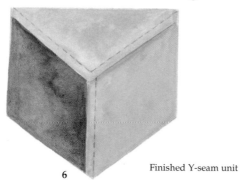

Finished Y-seam unit

6

**Half-star units:** With right sides together and raw edges even, and matching centre points exactly, pin one Y-seam unit to another. (The black diamond will be on top of a blue/purple diamond.) Stitch, remembering to back-stitch at seam allowance dots, and stopping and starting at dots (**Diagram 7**).

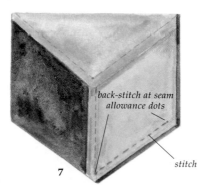

*back-stitch at seam allowance dots*

*stitch*

7

Pin and stitch a corner square to joined Y-seam units in same manner that was used to attach right-angle triangle. Press corner square seams towards diamonds, to complete a half-star unit (**Diagram 8**).

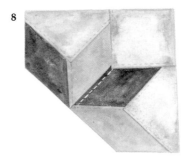

8

Finished half-star unit

**Completing Lemoyne Star blocks:** Matching raw edges and centre points, pin then stitch two half-star units together, stopping and starting at seam allowance dots. Attach two corner squares as before, pinning each point for accuracy. Press corner square seams towards star. All seam allowances on star will face the same direction and centre will turn and lie flat (**Diagram 9**). Make 20 star blocks in all.

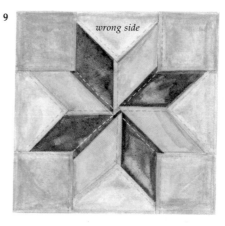

9

*wrong side*

Finished Lemoyne Star block

## Assembling Quilt Top

The blocks are set on point, so you will need to add setting blocks between the pieced blocks, and complete outer edges and each corner of the quilt with appropriate setting triangles.

From black fabric, cut 12 squares, each $10^1/2''$ (26.6cm), for setting blocks. Cut four squares, each $15^1/4''$ (39cm), then cut each square diagonally twice, to give 16 quarter-square triangles (there will be two spares) with the straight grain running along the long side of each triangle, for setting triangles. Also cut two squares, each 8" (20.2cm), then cut each square diagonally once, to give four half-square triangles with straight grain running along the right angle, for small setting triangles.

Referring to **Diagram 10**, and with right sides together, join blocks and setting triangles together to form rows. Press seams away from pieced blocks.

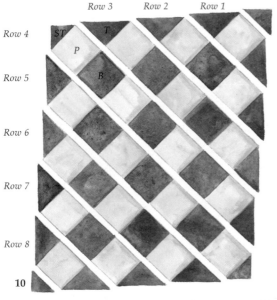

**10**

ST = small setting triangle    P = pieced (Lemoyne Star) block
T = setting triangle           B = setting block

**Rows 1 and 8:** Setting triangle, pieced block, setting triangle.

**Rows 2 and 7:** Setting triangle, pieced block, setting block, pieced block, setting triangle.

**Rows 3 and 6:** Setting triangle, pieced block, setting block, pieced block, setting block, pieced block, setting triangle.

**Row 4:** Small setting triangle, pieced block, setting block, pieced block, setting block, pieced block, setting block, pieced block, setting triangle.

**Row 5:** Setting triangle, pieced block, setting block, pieced block, setting block, pieced block, setting block, pieced block, setting triangle.

Stitch rows together, beginning at top right-hand corner. Stitch two remaining half-square triangles to outer edge of pieced block of Rows 1 and 8.

## Borders

**Inner border:** Measure length of quilt through centre of quilt top. From each of the 12 assorted fabrics, cut 2$^1$/$_2$" (6.3cm) strips of random length (6–20", or 15–51cm), and join to form side border strips that measure length of quilt top. With right sides together, stitch a border strip to each side of quilt top. Have border strip uppermost when stitching so that you can ease quilt top into size of border strip if necessary. Open out, and press seam allowances towards border strip. Repeat process to measure and join top and bottom border strips.

**Outer border:** From black fabric, cut a 4$^1$/$_2$yd (4m) length, for backing. From remaining fabric, cut four strips, each 6" (15.2cm) wide, along length of fabric. Measure length of quilt through centre of quilt top, and trim side border strips to this measurement. With right sides together, join a side border strip to either side of quilt. Measure width of quilt through centre of quilt top, trim remaining strips to this measurement and join to top and bottom of quilt.

## Quilting

Using one of the methods outlined in "Marking Quilting Patterns" on page 116, mark quilting lines on quilt top. You can follow our quilting design or quilt as desired. Our quilt has cobweb quilting on black setting squares and rainbow quilting on the outer border. These quilting patterns are printed on the pattern sheet.

Cut the 4$^1$/$_2$yd (4m) piece of black backing fabric in half lengthwise so that you have two pieces, and stitch together along 2$^1$/$_4$yd (2m) sides. Baste quilt top, batting and backing together, referring to "Layering Quilt" on page 116.

Referring to "Hand Quilting" on page 117, quilt along marked lines. We also outline quilted $^1$/$_4$" (6mm) from seam on Lemoyne Star blocks and inner border.

## Binding

Following directions for "Straight Binding: Double" on page 118, from the blue binding fabric, cut strips, join and apply to quilt edges.

Label and date your completed quilt.

*Part of the beauty of this quilt lies in the quilting, which shows up so well on the cream background ...*

# Dresden Plate Quilt

*Part of the great joy of quilting for many quiltmakers is the sense of companionship derived from*

*working on a shared project, tapping into a quilting tradition that has existed for centuries.*

*Dresden Plate is a great design for a group to make, because if the blocks do not*

*end up quite the same size, they can be trimmed without disturbing the pattern.*

*The petals can be made out of scraps, which even non-sewers can help to provide,*

*and the background fabric is inexpensive homespun.*

*The quilting pattern can be simplified, but remember that part of the beauty of this quilt*

*lies in the quilting, which shows up so well on the cream background.*

## MEASUREMENTS

Finished quilt measures 280cm x 235cm ($110^1/4''$ x $92^1/2''$).

## MATERIALS

- Assorted cotton prints, for petals (exact amounts are difficult to calculate, because of the odd shapes of individual pieces)
- Assorted fabrics in solid colours, for circles
- 10.5m x 115cm ($11^1/2$yds x 45") cream homespun, for background and borders
- 7.2m x 115cm (8yds x 45") coordinating fabric, for backing

- 1m x 115cm ($1^1/4$yds x 45") contrasting fabric, for binding
- Queen-size batting
- Coordinating machine thread
- Quilting thread
- Quilting needles (betweens)
- Template plastic or cardboard

## TEMPLATES

Templates for petal and circle are given on this page. Make two cardboard or plastic templates of both petal and circle, one of cutting line and one of sewing line. Mark midline on each petal template.

## CUTTING

Place cutting template on wrong side of fabric, trace around shape with a soft lead pencil and cut out. Centring sewing template on wrong side of each cut fabric shape, trace sewing line.

From assorted cotton prints, cut 444 petals (16 per plate plus 252 for border).

From solid colour fabrics, cut 12 circles.

From cream homespun, cut 12 squares, each 18" (46cm), for background blocks. (Cut the blocks in a single row along length of fabric and use remainder of fabric for top and bottom borders.)

Cut backing fabric into three $94^1/2$" (240cm) lengths.

## SEWING

### Dresden Plates

Carefully choose a combination of fabrics to make up a plate. Just one dark petal will look too strong — use two, three or four and position them symmetrically for balance. Avoid using only one very pale petal in a plate, because it will blend with the background and appear as a gap. Fabrics of similar tone are easiest to control.

With right sides together and stitching along sewing lines, join 16 petals along straight sides to make up a circle. Do not stitch through seam allowances at top and bottom of petal — these remain free. Press all seam allowances clockwise.

Position sewing template on right side of each petal and trace curved line of outer petal end. Baste seam allowances of curved ends under, ready for appliquéing to background block. Leave inner edges raw, as they will be covered by the circle.

Crease each background block into quarters, then centre a plate on the block, with creases running along petal midlines. Baste all edges to background fabric (see **Diagram**).

Clip across seam allowance to sewing line around each circle, press under allowance and baste to hold. Centre circle on top of each plate and baste in place. Using thread that blends with the print fabrics and referring to appliqué stitch diagram on page 119, hand-appliqué circles and plates in place. Take care not to catch backing fabric when appliquéing circles, as this fabric is cut away.

When appliqué is complete, carefully cut away the backing fabric from behind each plate, leaving a $^1/4$" (6mm) seam allowance (see photograph, page 15, below). This reduces bulk and leaves fewer layers for quilting. Make 12 blocks.

### Assembling Quilt Top

Lay the 12 blocks out on the floor to decide the most pleasing arrangement, then, with right sides together, join into four rows of three (allowing $^1/4$", or 6mm, seams). Join the rows, making sure the corners match. Press seam allowances to one side.

### Border and Scalloped Edge

Measure length of quilt top through centre of quilt. From homespun, cut two border strips, each $23^1/2$" (60cm) wide, to this measurement. With right sides together and border strip uppermost, join a strip to each long side of quilt top. Press seam allowances towards border strips. Repeat this process for top and bottom border strips, measuring width of quilt top through centre of quilt.

For scalloped edge, make 44 groups of five petals, and four groups of eight petals (latter will form corners of border). This time you will need to turn in the inner curved edges of petals as well as outer edges, as they will not be covered by circles.

For the side borders, join 13 of the groups of five, alternating them to give a sinuous effect (see photograph, right). Join nine groups for the top and bottom borders. Lay them out on the quilt with the four corner units and reposition them until they fit. You may have to take out one petal at each end of the side borders to make the corner turn properly. Once the border lies flat and even, baste it to the background, then hand-appliqué.

### Quilting

The pattern for quilting is given on the pattern sheet. Using one of the methods described in "Marking Quilting Patterns" on page 116, transfer quilting pattern onto cream background, placing centre of pattern at junction of four blocks, repeating half pattern at edges and extending grid lines to fill background, as desired.

To make up backing, join the three lengths along the grain and press. Following directions in "Layering Quilt" on page 116, baste quilt top, batting and backing together.

Following directions for "Hand Quilting" on page 117, outline quilt around each Dresden plate about $1/4$" (6mm) from seam lines, and then make an extra row $1/4$" from quilting lines, to puff up appliqué. Quilt pattern, as traced.

### Binding

Trim quilt edge into gently curved scallops, as shown in the photograph, above.

Following directions for "Bias Binding" on page 118, from binding fabric, make a continuous bias strip and apply to quilt edge, finishing by hand.

Sign and date your finished quilt.

*Be prepared to spend time on the quilting, as the heirloom-quality result will last for generations ...*

# Double
# Irish Chain
# Quilt

*This beautiful quilt has been assembled from fabric scraps and inexpensive calico — dozens of prints*

*and florals soften the overall effect of the Double Chain pattern, while the calico provides*

*the perfect background for the quilting. Be prepared to spend some time on the quilting,*

*as the heirloom-quality result will last for generations.*

## MEASUREMENTS

Finished quilt measures 171cm x 213cm ($67^1/_4$" x $84^3/_4$").

## MATERIALS

- 35 or more assorted printed medium and dark fabrics, each at least 13cm x 76cm (5" x 30"), for blocks

- 4.5m x 120cm (5yds x 47") calico, for blocks and border

- 3.6m x 115cm (4yds x 45") floral print, for backing

- 0.5m x 115cm ($^2/_3$yd x 45") printed fabric, for binding

- Queen-size batting

- Coordinating machine thread

- Quilting thread

- Quilting needles (betweens)

## SEWING

**Note:** $1/4''$ *(6mm) seam allowance is **included** in all measurements.*

### Block A

**Four-patch units:** From assorted printed fabrics, cut 86 strips, each $2^1/4''$ x 14" (5.7cm x 35.5cm).

With right sides facing, stitch two contrasting strips together (**Diagram 1a**). Open out strips, press seams towards darker fabric. Cut stitched strips across into $2^1/4''$ (5.7cm) segments (**Diagram 1b**). Arrange these segments into groups of two, mixing fabrics well, and stitch (**Diagram 1c**). Open out squares, press seams towards darker fabric.

Repeat this process to make 128 four-patch units. There will be one spare.

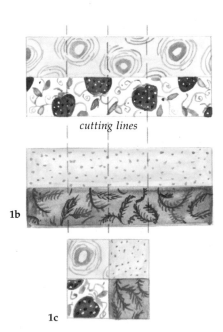

1a

*cutting lines*

1b

1c

**Two-patch units:** From assorted printed fabrics, cut 22 strips, each $2^1/4''$ x 14" (5.7cm x 35.5cm).

From calico, cut 22 strips, each $2^1/4''$ x 14" (5.7cm x 35.5cm).

With right sides facing, stitch a calico strip and printed fabric strip together (**Diagram 2a**). Open out strips and press seam allowances towards printed fabric. Cut stitched strips across into $2^1/4''$ (5.7cm) segments (**Diagram 2b**).

Repeat this process to make 128 two-patch units (**Diagram 2c**). There will be four spare.

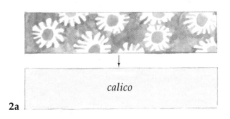

*calico*

2a

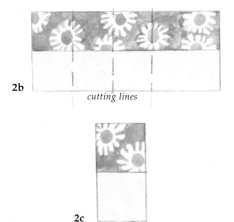

2b

*cutting lines*

2c

**Centres:** From assorted printed fabrics, cut 32 squares, each $2^1/4''$ (5.7cm), for centre of Block A.

**Completing Block A:** Join units of Block A together, as shown in **Diagram 3**, and continue until you have 32 blocks.

To avoid confusion during the piecing process, it's a good idea to sort the units into piles for each block before joining them together. This also gives you an opportunity to make sure you are satisfied with the overall arrangement of fabrics in each block; you are aiming for a good mix of fabrics.

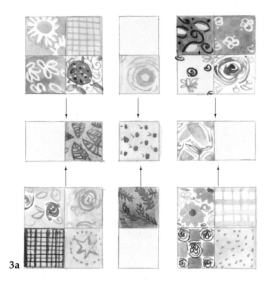

3a

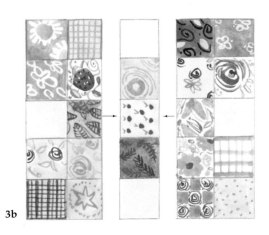

3b

3c

Finished Block A

## Block B

From assorted printed fabrics, cut 22 strips, each $2^1/_4$" x 14" (5.7cm x 35.5cm).

From calico, cut 11 strips, each $5^3/_4$" x 14" (14.5cm x 35.5cm).

With right sides together, join a printed fabric strip to each long side of a calico strip (**Diagram 4a**). Open out strips and press seam allowances towards calico. Cross-cut stitched strips into $2^1/_4$" (5.7cm) segments (**Diagram 4b**).

Repeat this process to make 62 units (**Diagram 4c**). There will be four spare.

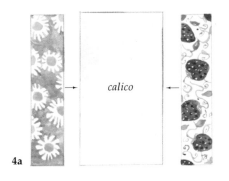

4a

4b

4c

From calico, cut four strips, each $5^3/_4$" x 47" (14.5cm x 120cm), and eight strips, each $2^1/_4$" x 47" (5.7cm x 120cm).

With right sides together, stitch a narrow strip to each long side of the wider strips. Open out narrow strips and press seam allowances away from wider strips. Cross-cut stitched strips into $5^3/_4$" (14.5cm) segments.

Repeat this process to make 31 units. There will be one spare.

Join units of Block B together, as shown in **Diagram 5**, and continue until you have 31 blocks.

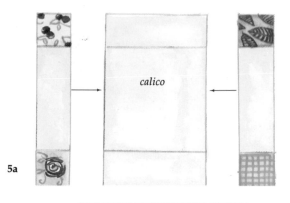

**5a**

**5b**

Finished Block B

## Assembling Quilt Top

Following the partial layout shown in **Diagram 6**, with right sides together, join Blocks A and B together in an alternating fashion into nine rows of seven blocks, taking care to match corners exactly. Press seam allowances towards Block B. Join rows together.

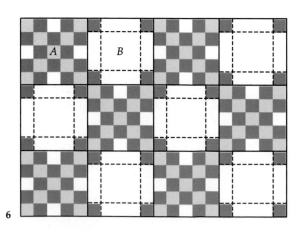

**6**

### Border

Place the quilt on a flat surface and measure length of quilt by measuring through centre of quilt top. From calico, cut two border strips, each $6^1/4''$ (15.8cm) wide, to this measurement.

Mark halves and quarters on both the border strips and the quilt top. With right sides together and half and quarter marks matching, join border strip to each long side of quilt top. When joining border strip to quilt top, have border strip uppermost so that it is easier to ease quilt top into size of border strip if measurements are a little different. Open out and press seam allowances towards border strip.

Repeat this process for top and bottom border strips, measuring width of quilt after side border strips have been attached.

### Quilting

Using one of the methods outlined in "Marking Quilting Patterns" on page 116, lightly mark quilting lines on quilt top. You can follow our quilting design or quilt as desired. We used a diagonal grid the width of each square on Block A and a flower with overlapping petals for centre of Block B. The border is quilted with an intertwined wave and central star motif. The quilting patterns for Block B and the border are printed on the pattern sheet. When tracing the border pattern, begin in the centre of each border strip and adjust the length of the wave just before each corner to achieve a smooth corner pattern.

Cut backing fabric in half lengthwise to give two pieces, each 72" x 45" (180cm x 115cm), and stitch two lengths together along 72" edge. Following directions in "Layering Quilt" on page 116, baste quilt top, batting and backing together. Hand or machine quilt, following pattern markings.

### Binding

Following directions for "Straight Binding: Double" on page 118, cut strips from binding fabric, join and apply to quilt edges.

Label and date your finished quilt.

Antique quilts were usually made from
necessity out of whatever fabrics
were available ...

# Antique Quilt
## c. 1900

*Antique quilts were usually made from necessity out of whatever fabrics were available. Yet, despite these practical constraints, many of the old quilts are very beautiful, reflecting the creativity and resourcefulness of their makers. Recreating this turn-of-the-century quilt will give you an opportunity to tap into this tradition — minus the need to "make do" with available materials (thank goodness for quilting shops!). The original quilt would have been pieced by hand, but your version can be quick-pieced on the machine. We have taken liberties with one of the blocks, redesigning it very slightly, as the original windblown design could only be hand-pieced. Oddly enough, this block appears only once; possibly the maker began with this block, decided it was too time consuming to repeat and didn't attempt it again!*

## MEASUREMENTS

Finished quilt measures approximately 220cm x 197cm (86$^1$/$_2$" x 77$^1$/$_2$").

## MATERIALS

◆ Mixture of light, medium and dark patterned and plain fabrics, 3m x 115cm (3$^1$/$_3$yds x 45") in total (see **Note**, page 24)

◆ 2.6m x 115cm (3yds x 45") pink checked fabric, for sashing and borders

◆ 0.8m x 115cm (1yd x 45") mustard checked fabric, for setting squares

◆ 230cm x 210cm (90$^1$/$_2$" x 83") batting

◆ 5m x 120cm (5$^1$/$_2$yds x 47") calico, for backing and binding

◆ Coordinating machine thread

◆ Quilting thread

◆ Quilting needles (betweens)

◆ Template plastic or cardboard

## SEWING

**Note:** *Our quilt is composed mainly of gingham, but striped, spotted, plaid and plain fabrics are also included. The sorts of plaid and check fabrics that can be found in men's workshirts would be suitable. Using "workmanlike" fabrics such as these, and inexpensive fabrics such as gingham, contributes to the effect of an antique, as well as making this an inexpensive quilt to produce.*

*$1/4$" (6mm) seam allowance is **included** in all measurements.*

### Block A

From a mixture of light, medium and dark patterned and plain fabrics, cut 20 squares, each $4^1/4$" (10.7cm), for quarter-square triangles.

From a mixture of checked fabrics, cut 20 squares, each $3^1/2$" (8.8cm), for setting squares.

From contrasting plain or striped fabrics, cut five squares, each $3^1/2$" (8.8cm), for centre squares.

From a mixture of contrasting checked fabrics, cut 20 strips, each $2^3/4$" x $9^1/2$" (7cm x 24cm), for sashing.

From other contrasting checked fabrics, cut 20 squares, each $2^3/4$" (7cm), for corners.

Sort $4^1/4$" squares into separate piles of light, medium and dark fabrics. Referring to diagrams and instructions for half-square triangle units on page 115, join contrasting squares from different piles to make 20 half-square triangle units.

Following instructions for quick-piecing quarter-square triangles on page 116, join new half-square triangle units together, to form 20 quarter-square triangle units in all.

With right sides facing, stitch setting squares, centre square and quarter-square triangle units together to form a nine-patch block, following sequence shown in **Diagram 1**.

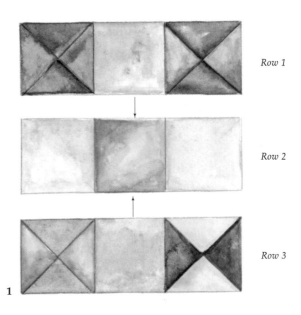

*Row 1*

*Row 2*

*Row 3*

1

**Row 1:** Quarter-square triangle unit, setting square, quarter-square triangle unit.
**Row 2:** Setting square, centre square, setting square.
**Row 3:** Quarter-square triangle unit, setting square, quarter-square triangle unit.

Repeat this procedure, using a good mix of fabrics, until you have five nine-patch blocks.

Stitch a sashing strip to each side of the five nine-patch blocks; you will have 10 strips remaining. Stitch a corner square to each end of the remaining sashing strips, then stitch one of these strips to the top and bottom of each block to form five completed A blocks (**Diagram 2**).

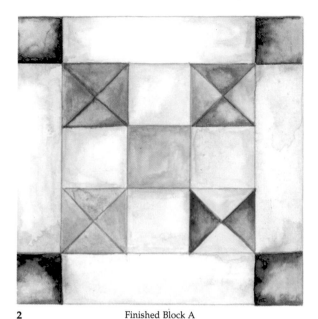

**2**        Finished Block A

The finished blocks should be 13$^1$/$_2$″ (34.2cm) square.

## Block B

From a mixture of light, medium and dark fabrics, cut 160 squares, each 3$^5$/$_8$″ (9.2cm), for half-square triangle units.

From a mixture of contrasting checked fabrics, cut 40 strips, each 2$^3$/$_4$″ x 6″ (7cm x 15.2cm), for sashing.

From plaid or striped fabric, cut 10 squares, each 2$^3$/$_4$″ (7cm), for centre squares.

Sort 3$^5$/$_8$″ squares into separate piles of light, medium and dark fabrics. Referring to diagrams and instructions for quick-piecing half-square triangle units on page 115, join contrasting squares from different piles to make 160 half-square triangle units.

Sort half-square triangle units into as many matching groups of four as possible. The remainder will be mismatched, for a scrap effect. With right sides together, stitch four matching half-square triangle units together to form a diamond within a square (**Diagram 3**). Continue until you have 40 units.

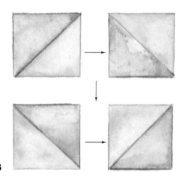

**3**

With right sides together, stitch a pieced diamond within a square to a sashing strip, then stitch another pieced diamond within a square — a matching one, if possible — to the other side of the strip (**Diagram 4**). Continue joining pieced squares and strips in this manner until you have 20 pieced units.

**4**

Join the remaining sashing strips to either side of the 2$^3$/$_4$″ (7cm) centre squares, to make 10 pieced strips.

Join a matching pieced unit to either side of a pieced strip, to form the completed B block (**Diagram 5**), which should be $13^1/2''$ (34.2cm) square.

5              Finished Block B

Repeat this procedure, aiming to have pieced units composed of identical half-square triangles within the same block, with an occasional mismatched unit, to make 10 B blocks.

## Block C

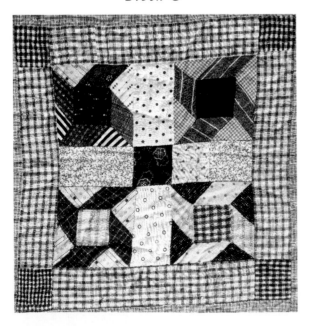

Block C (there is only one) is made up of four windblown blocks joined together by sashing strips. The windblown blocks in the original quilt have been pieced by hand, allowing the stitcher to work miracles with the mitred corners. To enable these blocks to be stitched by machine, we have adapted them so that each block consists of pieced triangles rather than parallelograms.

The triangle templates — one of cutting line and one of sewing line — for the windblown block are printed below. Make a template of each.

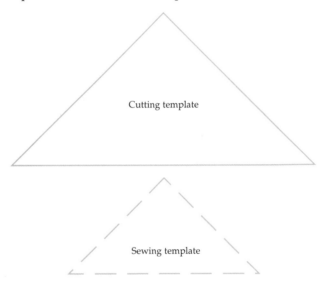

When cutting, place cutting template on wrong side of chosen fabric, trace around shape and cut out. Centre sewing template on each cut triangle, and trace sewing line onto wrong side of fabric.

From 13 light, medium and dark fabrics, cut 48 triangles, cutting even numbers of triangles from the same fabric. From each of four different fabrics, cut a $2^1/2''$ (6.3cm) square — four for windblown block centres and one for centre square of Block C.

From each of four different light fabrics, cut a strip, $2^1/2'' \times 4^1/2''$ (6.3cm x 11.4cm), for sashing.

From checked fabric, cut four strips, each $2^1/4'' \times 10^1/2''$ (5.7cm x 26.6cm), for framing.

From a contrasting checked fabric, cut four squares, each $2^1/4''$ (5.7cm), for corners.

With right sides together, stitch a triangle to each side of the block centres, noting that corners of triangles extend beyond edges of squares, and joining either two or four same-fabric triangles to each centre block, to make four centre diamonds (**Diagram 6**).

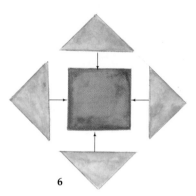

6

Stitch two contrasting triangles together along one of their shorter sides, ensuring left-hand triangle in the pair matches one of the triangles stitched to one of the centre squares in the previous step. Repeat with remaining triangles, using same-fabric triangles on same sides of the units, to form four bi-coloured triangles per windblown block, or 16 in total (**Diagram 7**).

7

Join a bi-coloured triangle to each side of a centre diamond (**Diagram 8**).

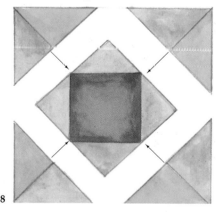

8

Repeat this procedure, matching triangles in order to create a windblown pattern, to make four windblown blocks in all (**Diagram 9**).

9

Finished windblown block

With right sides together, stitch a windblown block to one side of a sashing strip, then stitch another block to the other side. Repeat this procedure, then join the remaining sashing strips to either side of the centre square, to form a pieced strip. Arrange the rows, placing the pieced strip in the middle, and stitch.

With right sides together, stitch a framing strip to either side of the pieced block. Join a corner square to each end of two remaining strips, then stitch these strips to the top and bottom of the block, to form the completed C block (**Diagram 10**). It should be $13^1/_2$" (34.2cm) square.

10

Finished Block C

## Assembling Quilt Top

From pink checked fabric, cut 32 strips, each 7" x 14" (17.8cm x 35.5cm), for sashing.

From mustard checked fabric, cut 15 setting squares, each 7" (17.8cm).

Arrange the 16 pieced blocks into four rows of four. With right sides together, join the four pieced blocks in each row, by stitching a sashing strip in between each pieced block. Press seam allowances towards pieced blocks.

Arrange the remaining sashing strips into five rows of four. With right sides together, join the four sashing strips in each row by stitching a mustard setting square in between each strip. Press seam allowances towards setting squares.

Refer to **Diagram 11** when assembling quilt top. Join a pieced strip to the top edge of each four-block strip, then join all rows together, matching seam lines accurately (seams should lock together). Join the remaining pieced strip to the bottom edge of the quilt.

## Side Borders

From remaining pink checked fabric, cut $2^1/_2$" (6.3cm) strips across width of fabric. Measure the length of your quilt through the centre of the quilt top and join strips to form two side border strips, each measuring length of quilt top.

With right sides together and with border strip uppermost, stitch a border strip to either side of quilt top, easing quilt top into border strip if necessary.

## Quilting

Using one of the methods outlined in "Marking Quilting Patterns" on page 116, lightly mark quilting lines on quilt top. The original quilt has been quilted with an overlapping rainbow pattern. If you wish to quilt this pattern, the border pattern for the Lemoyne Star Quilt, printed on the pattern sheet, could be used as a basis. Otherwise, quilt as desired.

From calico, cut two lengths, each $2^3/_4$yds x 45" (2.5m x 115cm). Cut one in half lengthwise and stitch one half-length to each side of remaining length of

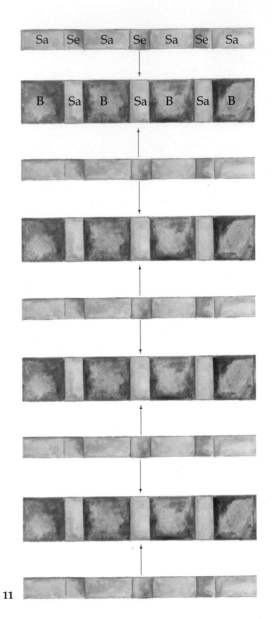

11

Se = setting square
B = pieced block
Sa = sashing strip

backing fabric. Following directions in "Layering Quilt" on page 116, baste quilt top, batting and backing together. Do not trim backing at this stage.

Referring to "Hand Quilting" on page 117, quilt along marked lines.

## Binding

Bind the quilt, following instructions for "Self-binding — Back to Front" on page 117.

Label and date your completed quilt.

*Birds in the Fountain*

# QUILTS *for* Hanging

*While all the quilts within this book look good, some display such uniquely decorative qualities as to demand to be hung. Here is our selection for the gallery: two traditional wall-hangings featuring classic floral motifs, a naïve doll quilt, a folk-art-inspired flannel quilt with a pieced central cabin motif, and a vibrantly coloured child's quilt that takes appliqué into a new dimension.*

*These naïve dollies seem to dance in celebration of their country charm ...*

# Naïve Doll Quilt

*With their checked pinafores and knotted locks, these naïve dollies seem to dance*

*in celebration of their country charm. They're adaptable as well as cute, and could easily be*

*reincarnated as a set of matching cushion covers to brighten a chair or sofa.*

*For this is essentially a lighthearted quilt — full of whimsy and fun to make.*

## MEASUREMENTS

Finished quilt measures approximately 107cm x 136cm ($42^1/_4$" x $53^1/_2$").

## MATERIALS

18cm (7") square of each of 12 different plaid fabrics, for dresses

0.5m x 115cm ($^2/_3$yd x 45") gingham, for hands and feet

0.5m x 115cm ($^2/_3$yd x 45") black fabric, for heads

0.7m x 115cm ($^3/_4$yd x 45") light printed fabric, for aprons and background blocks

1.5m x 115cm ($1^2/_3$yds x 45") plaid fabric, for hearts and backing

1.3m x 115cm ($1^1/_2$yds x 45") dark printed fabric, for setting blocks and triangles, and outer border

0.6m x 115cm ($^2/_3$yd x 45") plain contrasting fabric, for inner border and binding

150cm (60") square of cotton batting

Black stranded embroidery cotton, for hair

Beads to decorate hair (optional)

Coordinating machine thread

Quilting thread

Quilting needles (betweens)

## APPLIQUÉ OUTLINES

Before proceeding, read through "Traditional Appliqué Method 1" on page 114. All appliqué outlines are printed on the pattern sheet and labelled with the letter A. Trace onto paper 12 dresses, 24 hands, 24 feet, 12 aprons, 12 heads and four hearts.

## CUTTING

When cutting appliqué shapes, remember to **add** $^1/_4$" (6mm) seam allowance all round. $^1/_4$" (6mm) seam allowance is **included** in all other measurements.

From light printed fabric, cut 12 squares, each $8^1/_2$" (21.5cm), for background blocks.

From dark printed fabric, cut six squares, each $8^1/_2$" (21.5cm), for setting blocks. Cut also three squares, each $12^1/_2$" (31.8cm), then cut each square diagonally twice (four quarter-square triangles), for setting triangles. You will have 12 triangles in all — including two spares. For small corner setting triangles, cut two squares, each 6" (15.2cm). Cut each square diagonally once only, giving four half-square triangles in all. Reserve the remaining fabric for the outer border.

From plain contrasting fabric, cut five $2^1/_4$" (5.7cm) strips across width of fabric, for binding. Reserve the remaining fabric for the inner border.

## SEWING

### Appliqué and Embroidery

Find and mark centre of each appliqué block by pressing block in quarters diagonally. Referring to photograph on page 35, appliqué all pieces into position, following directions for "Traditional Appliqué Method 1" and sequence outlined below.

First, position dress on appliqué block, matching centre marks on dress with centre of block, then tuck under hands and feet. Baste and appliqué dress, hands and feet in place. Position apron on dress, using centre marks as a guide. Baste and appliqué in place. There is no need to turn and baste the seam allowance on straps of apron, as raw edges will be covered by doll's head. Position the head so that it covers raw edges of apron, baste and appliqué in place.

Position hearts on small corner setting triangles, and appliqué in place.

Mark seven evenly spaced dots around each doll's head for position of hair tufts. Using six strands of embroidery cotton, sew four or five $^1/_2$" (1.2cm) loops for each tuft, taking a small back-stitch after making each loop to anchor it. To finish each tuft, wind thread twice around base of loops, take needle through to back of fabric and secure thread. Cut through tops of loops and trim to desired length. Continue until all 12 blocks are complete. Decorate tufts with beads, if desired.

### Assembling Quilt Top

The blocks are set on point, so you will need to add setting blocks between the pieced blocks, and complete outer edges and each corner of the quilt with appropriate setting triangles.

Referring to the **Diagram** below, with right sides together, join blocks and setting triangles together to form rows. Press seams away from pieced blocks.

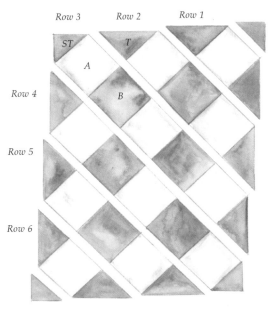

ST = small setting triangle    A = appliqué block
T = setting triangle    B = setting block

**Rows 1 and 6:** Setting triangle, appliqué block, setting triangle.
**Rows 2 and 5:** Setting triangle, appliqué block, setting block, appliqué block, setting triangle.

**Row 3:** Small setting triangle, appliqué block, setting block, appliqué block, setting block, appliqué block, setting triangle.

**Row 4:** Setting triangle, appliqué block, setting block, appliqué block, setting block, appliqué block, small setting triangle.

Stitch rows together, beginning with Row 1 and working towards Row 6. Stitch two remaining small setting triangles to outer edge of appliqué block of Rows 1 and 6.

### Borders

**Inner border:** Measure length of quilt, through the centre of quilt top. From plain contrasting fabric, cut two border strips, each $1^3/4''$ (4.5cm) wide, to this measurement. With right sides together and border strip uppermost, stitch a strip to each side of quilt top. Open out, and press seam allowances towards border strips. Repeat this process for top and bottom border strips, measuring width of quilt after side border strips have been attached.

**Outer border:** Measure length of quilt again, then, from dark printed fabric, cut two $3^1/4''$ (8.2cm) strips to this measurement. (You may need to join strips to achieve this length.) Join strips to sides of quilt top, following directions for inner border. Repeat process to join top and bottom border strips.

### Quilting

Mark outline for quilted heart in centre of each apron (refer to apron appliqué outline for placement) and outline for larger heart in centre of each setting block and triangle (use appliqué heart outline as template). Note that points on quilted hearts on triangles all face towards centre of quilt top, and points on quilted hearts on setting blocks all face towards bottom of quilt. At top left-hand and bottom right-hand corner, mark a diagonal

line from outer corner to inside corner of inner border. Using these lines as guides, continue to mark evenly spaced diagonal lines along borders (there will be about $1^1/8''$, or 2.8cm, between rows).

Referring to "Layering Quilt" on page 116, baste quilt top, batting and backing together.

Outline quilt around each appliqué piece. Quilt another row around each doll's body, feet and hands. Quilt heart in centre of each apron. Quilt heart on each setting block and triangle, then quilt another row, allowing $^1/4''$ (6mm) between rows. Quilt along marked diagonal lines.

### Binding

Following directions in "Straight Binding: Double" on page 118, join binding strips and apply to edges of quilt.

Label and date your finished quilt.

## APPLIQUÉ OUTLINES

Before proceeding, read through "Traditional Appliqué Method 1" on page 114. All appliqué outlines are printed full size on the pattern sheet and labelled with the letter B. Trace onto paper one fountain, one top fountain trim, one bottom fountain trim, one large star, one small star, two vases, two vase trims, three petals and three each of centres 1 and 2 for left-hand posy, five buds for right-hand posy, 13 small leaves for posies, one large bird 1 and one large bird 2, one small bird 1 and one small bird 2, 60 water droplets, two butterflies, 48 large leaves, and 24 each of flower circles 1, 2 and 3 and flower centre, for border garland. Note that some shapes, such as the large birds, consist of overlapping pieces. Trace all pieces.

## CUTTING

When cutting appliqué shapes from fabric, remember to **add** $^1/_4$" (6mm) seam allowance. There is no need to add seam allowance to fountain top and base and base of vases, as a contrasting trim is appliquéd over raw edges. $^1/_4$" (6mm) seam allowance is **included** in all other measurements.

From dark green printed fabric, cut four bias strips, each $1^1/_4$" x 6" (3cm x 15.2cm), for posy stems.

From medium green printed fabric, cut $1^1/_2$" (3.7cm) bias strips, for garland stem. Join to form a length of approximately $4^1/_4$yds (3.8m).

From cream fabric, cut two $1^1/_3$yd (1.2m) lengths. From one length, cut a 26" (66cm) square, for the centre block; this is trimmed to $24^1/_2$" (62cm) when appliqué is complete. From remaining length, cut two strips, each $24^1/_2$" x 8" (62cm x 20.2cm), for side borders, and two strips, each $40^1/_2$" x 8" (103cm x 20.2cm), for top and bottom borders. Cut also a 45" (115cm) square, for backing.

From deep red fabric, cut four strips, each $24^1/_2$" x $1^3/_4$" (62cm x 4.5cm), for sawtooth edging.

## SEWING

### Centre Block

Find and mark the centre of the centre block by folding it twice diagonally, then fold side to side and top to bottom. Use the folded lines on the centre block and the photograph on page 36 as a guide, and refer to "Traditional Appliqué Method 1", when appliquéing shapes to background fabric. Leave a reasonable border around the design so that the centre block can be trimmed.

Position fountain on the centre block, approximately $1^1/_4$" (3cm) down from the horizontal centre line. Baste then appliqué fountain to background fabric along the sides. Baste then appliqué top fountain trim in place, covering raw edge of fountain with bottom edge of trim. Repeat this procedure for the bottom fountain trim. Position stars on the fountain, then baste and appliqué them in place.

Pin vases in position. Lightly trace posy outlines (on pattern sheet) onto background fabric. Pin posy petals and buds in position. Pin birds' bodies and wings in position above fountain. Adjust position of the petal and bird on left-hand side, if necessary. The bird's feet should rest comfortably on the petal and its beak should rest on top of the fountain. Appliqué birds' bodies and wings, then appliqué or embroider — using two strands of embroidery cotton and stem stitch (see page 119) — birds' legs in place. Appliqué a fabric eye on each bird and work buttonhole stitch (see page 119) around the edge, using two strands of contrasting thread.

With wrong sides together, finger-press bias strips for posy stems in half along their length, and machine baste $^1/_8$" (3mm) from raw edges. Pin bias stems in position on appliqué background, with basting line on each stem strip running along one stem outline and raw edges facing towards centre of stem outline (**Diagram 1**). Trim ends, tuck ends of stem $^1/_4$" (6mm) under tops of vases and under petals or buds. Work a running stitch next to basting line.

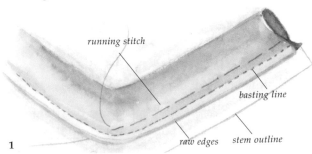

*running stitch*

*basting line*

**1**

*raw edges*   *stem outline*

Fold stem strip back over raw edges, finger-press and ease or stretch fabric as necessary to give a smooth, flat seam. Baste then appliqué stitch folded edge in place.

Baste then appliqué small posy leaves in position.

Baste then appliqué petals above left-hand vase, then appliqué flower centres 1 and 2. Baste vase in position, then appliqué. Baste each vase trim in place, folding bottom edge of trim over raw edge of vase and appliqué stitching in place.

Baste then appliqué water droplets in position. Note that the seam allowance on the water drops acts as padding.

Baste and appliqué small birds 1 and 2 in place. Using two strands of embroidery cotton, work a bullion stitch (see page 119) for the birds' eyes.

Baste and appliqué butterflies' wings in position. Baste and appliqué bodies over wings. Using two strands of embroidery cotton and back-stitch, embroider antennae. Work a bullion stitch for the butterflies' eyes.

### Sawtooth Edging

Trim appliquéd centre block so that it is exactly 24$^1$/$_2$″ (62cm) square.

With raw edges even and wrong side of sawtooth edging strip facing right side of border strip, stitch sawtooth strip to a border strip. Machine baste the sawtooth strip to the border strip $^1$/$_4$″ (6mm) from the outer edge of the sawtooth strip (**Diagram 2**).

Mark the centre of the inner edge of the sawtooth strip and 12″ (30.4cm) on either side. Starting $^1$/$_4$″ (6mm) from the end of the sawtooth strip, draw lines across width of strip at 2″ (5cm) intervals (**Diagram 3**).

On the outer edge, push back the raw edge to the machine basting and mark small dots on the outer border fabric, halfway between the marked lines (**Diagram 4**).

Unpick about 3″ (7.5cm) of the machine basting and carefully cut along the first marked line, almost to the inner edge of stitching, leaving only a couple of threads of fabric uncut (**Diagram 5**).

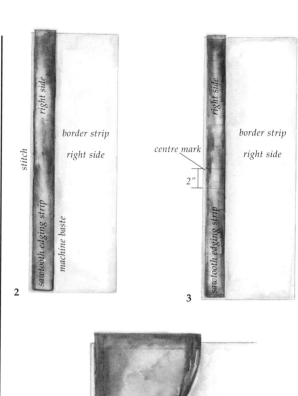

2

3

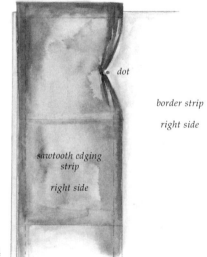

4

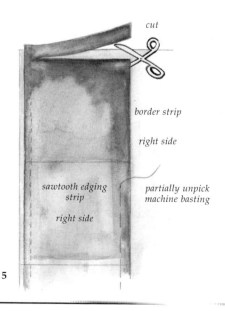

5

Finger-press the sawtooth fabric under to the small dot on the outer border to form one side of the triangle (**Diagram 6**).

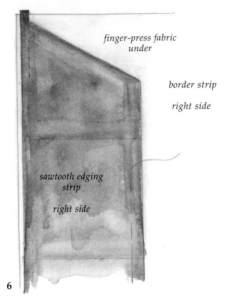

finger-press fabric under

border strip

*right side*

sawtooth edging strip

*right side*

6

Trim excess fabric, then appliqué from the inner border to the dot on the outer border. Fold under the sharp point, turn and appliqué the other side to form a triangle (**Diagram 7**).

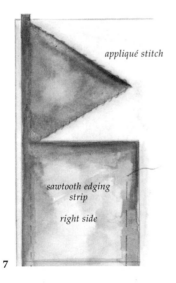

appliqué stitch

sawtooth edging strip

*right side*

7

Take a couple of extra stitches at the "V" on the inner border to prevent fraying.

Repeat until all 12 triangles are completed.

Using the same procedure, make another three sawtooth strips, to complete sawtooth edging.

### Border

With right sides together and matching ends and centres, stitch a side border strip to either side of centre block, stitching over the row of machine stitching on the inner edge of the border strip, but taking care that the "V"s of the sawtooth edging are not covered. Attach top and bottom border strips in the same manner.

Referring to the photograph on page 36, lightly sketch in the outline of the stem for the border garland. Appliqué bias stem in place, using the method outlined for the posy stems on the centre block (see page 38).

Baste and appliqué garland flowers in place, building up petal layers from largest to smallest flower centre. Distribute the flower highlights randomly around the garland. Baste and appliqué large leaves into position along the stem, using your eye to place them randomly.

### Quilting

Using one of the methods outlined in "Marking Quilting Patterns" on page 116, mark quilting lines on quilt top. Using the sawtooth edging as a guide, mark a diagonal grid on the background of the centre block (avoiding the appliquéd shapes), and continue a diagonal line to each corner of the quilt. Also mark a straight line from the tip of each triangle in the sawtooth edging to the outer edge of the quilt. Continue these straight lines at 2" (5cm) intervals into the corners so that they intersect the corner diagonals (see photograph, opposite).

Baste quilt top, batting and backing together, following directions in "Layering Quilt" on page 116. Referring to "Hand Quilting" on page 117, quilt along marked lines. Our quilt was also outline quilted around all shapes, with an extra row around the garland in the border.

### Binding

Following directions for "Straight Binding: Double" on page 118, cut enough strips from binding fabric to go around edge of quilt, join and apply to quilt edges.

Label and date your completed quilt.

*Detail of corner quilting pattern*

*Easy to appliqué and quick to piece,
the perfect project for the less
experienced stitcher ...*

# Country Vase with Flowers

*The vase of flowers motif often makes an appearance in traditional appliqué,*

*but here it plays a starring role — in strong colours and surrounded by a simple border*

*of flying geese. Easy to appliqué and quick to piece, this wall-hanging is the*

*perfect project for the less experienced stitcher.*

## MEASUREMENTS

Finished quilt measures approximately 72.5cm (28$^1$/$_2$") square.

## MATERIALS

- 1m x 115cm (1$^1$/$_3$yds x 45") cream fabric, for appliqué background and flying geese background

- 0.7m x 115cm (³/₄yd x 45") red check fabric, for vase and flying geese

- 0.5m x 115cm (²/₃yd x 45") dark green print, for stems and binding

- Small amount each of red, yellow and blue floral prints, for flowers and buds

- 0.2m x 115cm (¹/₄yd x 45") green check fabric, for leaves

- 0.2m x 115cm (¹/₄yd x 45") dark red fabric, for framing and vase shadows

- 1m x 115cm (1$^1$/$_4$yds x 45") dark red check fabric, for backing

- 86cm (34") square of batting

- Coordinating machine thread

- Quilting thread

- Quilting needles (betweens)

## APPLIQUÉ OUTLINES

Before proceeding, read through "Traditional Appliqué Method 1" on page 114. The appliqué design outline is printed full-size on the pattern sheet. Lightly trace design onto background fabric. Trace onto paper one vase plus two vase handle shadows, 10 leaves, two buds (two shapes per bud), three large flowers (four circles per flower), two medium flowers (three circles per flower) and two small flowers (two circles per flower).

## CUTTING

When cutting appliqué shapes, remember to **add** $1/4$" (6mm) seam allowance before cutting. $1/4$" (6mm) seam allowance is **included** in all other measurements.

From dark green print, cut three bias strips, each $1^1/4$" x 9" (3cm x 22.7cm), for longer stems, and six strips, each $1^1/4$" x 6" (3cm x 22.7cm), for shorter stems.

From cream fabric, cut a 21" (53.5cm) square, for appliqué background (this is a generous measurement; trim to $19^1/2$" (49.5cm) when appliqué is complete), and 96 squares, each $2^1/2$" (6.3cm), for flying geese backgrounds.

From dark red fabric, cut two strips, each 1" x $19^1/2$" (2.5cm x 49.5cm), for side frames, and two strips, each 1" x $20^1/2$" (2.5cm x 52cm), for top and bottom frames.

From red check fabric, cut 48 rectangles, each $2^1/2$" x $4^1/2$" (6.3cm x 11.4cm), for flying geese.

From backing fabric, cut a 34" (86.5cm) square.

## SEWING

### Appliqué

Use the photograph on page 45 as a guide and refer to "Traditional Appliqué Method 1" when appliquéing shapes to background fabric.

Baste vase in position. With wrong sides together, finger-press bias strips for stems in half along their length, then machine baste a scant $1/8$" (3mm) from raw edges. Pin bias stems in position on appliqué background, with basting line on each stem strip

running along one marked outline of stem and raw edges facing towards centre of stem outline. Trim ends of stems, then tuck under top of vase. Work a running stitch next to basting line, sewing closer to folded edge for thinner stems (see **Diagram**). Trim seam allowances, fold stem strip back over raw edges, finger-pressing and easing or stretching fabric as necessary to give a smooth, flat seam. Baste then appliqué stitch folded edge in place.

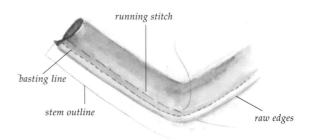

*running stitch*

*basting line*

*stem outline*

*raw edges*

Appliqué vase, then baste and appliqué shadows on handles.

Baste then appliqué flowers and buds, covering raw ends of stems and building up layers of flowers by appliquéing largest circle first. Baste then appliqué leaves in position.

### Frame

Trim appliquéd centre block so that it is exactly $19^1/2$" (49.5cm) square.

Mark centres of sides of appliquéd block and centres of side frames. Matching centre marks and with right sides together, join a side framing strip to each side of appliquéd block. Open out, and press seam allowances towards framing strips. Repeat to join top and bottom framing strips.

Framed centre block should measure $20^1/2$" (52cm), including seam allowances.

### Flying Geese Border

Referring to instructions for quick-piecing flying geese units on page 115, and using the red check fabric for the flying geese and the cream fabric for the background squares, make 48 flying geese units. Accurate piecing is important here; the border strips formed from the joined units need to fit the framed centre block.

*Appliquéd centre block*

Join 10 geese units for each side border, and 14 units for top and bottom borders.

With right sides together and border strip uppermost, join a side border strip to either side of framed centre block; ease strip to fit, if necessary. Repeat this process to join top and bottom borders.

## Quilting

Mark quilting lines on quilt top using preferred method (see "Marking Quilting Patterns" on page 116). You can follow our quilting pattern or quilt as desired. A diagonal grid has been quilted over the background square (avoiding the appliqué pieces). Mark equal intervals along the sides of the background square (there should be a little over 2" (5cm) between each mark), and join marks diagonally.

Following directions in "Layering Quilt" on page 116, baste quilt top, batting and backing together.

Referring to "Hand Quilting" on page 117, outline quilt around appliqué pieces and flying geese, then quilt along marked lines.

## Binding

Following directions in "Straight Binding: Double" on page 118, cut enough strips from binding fabric to go around quilt, join and apply to edges of quilt.

Label and date your finished quilt.

*This cosy quilt would look great as a wall-hanging, but is more likely to find its way to a favourite armchair ...*

# Cabin Flannel Quilt

*With its central cabin motif and cotton flannel patches, this unpretentious quilt*

*embodies all the warmth and comforts of home. While it would look great as a wall hanging,*

*it's more likely to find its way to a favourite armchair — and it would make a wonderful throw.*

## MEASUREMENTS

Finished quilt measures approximately 143cm (56$^1$/$_4$″) square.

## MATERIALS

- Small amount each of assorted cotton flannels (including a pale solid colour for background and a dark green print for tree tops), for centre block (see **Note**, page 48)

- 0.3m x 115cm ($^1$/$_3$yd x 45″) each of approximately 24 light, medium and dark cotton flannels, for sugar bowl panel and hourglass border (see **Note**, page 48)

- 0.3m x 115cm ($^1$/$_3$yd x 45″) brown cotton flannel ticking, for inner frame

- 0.4m x 115cm ($^1$/$_2$yd x 45″) solid red cotton flannel, for outer frame and binding

- 0.5m x 115cm ($^2$/$_3$yd x 45″) red checked cotton flannel, for inner border and outer border

- 3.3m x 115cm (3$^2$/$_3$yds x 45″) coordinating cotton flannel, for backing

- 170cm (67″) square of cotton or polyester batting

- Coordinating machine thread

- Brown perle cotton No. 8

- Quilting needles (betweens)

**1**

**KEY:**

A = 2¹/₂″ x 4¹/₂″ (6.3cm x 11.4cm)   D = 2¹/₂″ x 10¹/₂″ (6.3cm x 26.6cm)   G = 1¹/₂″ x 1¹/₂″ (3.7cm x 3.7cm)   J = 2″ x 7″ (5cm x 17.8cm)

B = 2¹/₂″ x 2¹/₂″ (6.3cm x 6.3cm)   E = 2″ x 10¹/₂″ (5cm x 26.6cm)   H = 1″ x 2″ (2.5cm x 5cm)   K = 1″ x 2¹/₂″ (2.5cm x 6.3cm)

C = 1¹/₂″ x 2¹/₂″ (3.7cm x 6.3cm)   F = 1¹/₂″ x 3″ (3.7cm x 7.5cm)   I = 1¹/₂″ x 2″ (3.7cm x 5cm)

**Note:** *Use fewer fabrics if you wish. It's a good idea not to use too many of the fabrics that appear in the centre block in the rest of the quilt in order to keep the centre block distinct. It is also important that all patches are cut accurately, and therefore we recommend that you use a rotary cutter and quilter's ruler (refer to "Rotary Cutting" on page 114).*

*¹/₄″ (6mm) seam allowance is **included** in all the given measurements*

## SEWING

### Centre Block

Refer to **Diagram 1** when cutting the patches for the centre block. Patches cut to the same size are identified by a letter (see accompanying key), and patches cut from the same fabric are coloured the same and identified by a number. (Note that same-sized patches are not necessarily cut from the same fabric.)

*Join patches together to form
rows, then join rows together
to form completed block*

*Use quick-piecing method for
flying geese units to create
accurate right-angle triangles
on either end of roof section*

2

From Fabric 1 (red check), cut one A patch and two C patches.

From Fabric 2 (pale check), cut five B patches.

From Fabric 3 (grey stripe), cut two A patches, eight C patches, one D patch and one E patch. Make sure stripes run in same direction.

From Fabric 4 (dark grey), cut one D patch and two H patches.

From Fabric 5 (solid beige), cut one A patch, four B patches, 48 G patches and four I patches.

From Fabric 6 (green print), cut 24 F patches.

From Fabric 7 (floral print), cut two J patches.

From each of Fabrics 8, 9 and 10 (two checks and one ticking), cut one K patch.

Piece the house in sections, following the sequence shown in **Diagram 2.**

Note that the roof section is a modified flying geese unit. Attach a solid beige B patch to either end of a dark grey D patch, following directions for quick-piecing flying geese units on page 115. The result should be two accurate right-angle triangles.

Once the house is complete, piece the 24 pine tree tops. Each pine tree top is a modified flying geese unit consisting of an F patch and two G patches. Use the quick-piecing method (as for the roof section) on page 115.

Join a pieced trunk section to each pine tree (**Diagram 3**), then join a pieced pine tree border to each side of house. Press seam allowances towards house.

Piece steps (K patches) together, stitch a lawn (J patch) to either side, then join completed section to house and trees.

The completed centre block should measure $15^1/2''$ (39.3cm) square, including seam allowances.

### Frames

**Note:** *Measure the centre block (through the centre) before cutting framing strips. It's likely that it will be smaller than the measurement given above; if so, cut framing strips a little wider to make up the difference. It's important that the quilt top is large enough to accommodate sugar bowl panels.*

**Inner frame:** From brown ticking, cut two strips, each $1^1/2''$ x $15^1/2''$ (3.7cm x 39.3cm), for side framing strips, and two strips, each $1^1/2''$ x $17^1/2''$ (3.7cm x 44.5cm), for top and bottom framing strips.

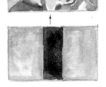

**3**

With right sides together, join a side framing strip to either side of centre block. Have strip uppermost when stitching so that you can ease or stretch the centre block to fit if necessary. Repeat the process to join the remaining strips to top and bottom of centre block. Press seam allowances towards frame.

**Outer frame:** From solid red flannel, cut two strips, each 2" x $17^1/2''$ (5cm x 44.5cm), for side framing strips, and two strips, each 2" x $20^1/2''$ (5cm x 52cm), for top and bottom framing strips.

Join a side framing strip to either side of the centre block, then stitch the remaining strips to top and bottom edges of block. Press seam allowances towards frame.

The framed centre block should measure $20^1/2''$ (52cm) square, including seam allowances.

### Sugar Bowl Panel

The sugar bowl panel is made up of 12 blocks, with each block consisting of four quarter-circles set in the centre of a four-square block, and with each element in a different fabric.

Choose 24 fabrics and arrange them into 12 pairs of complementary colours.

From one of the fabrics in a pair, cut an 11" (27.8cm) background square.

A full-size outline of the circle template is printed on page 52. Make 12 paper templates.

Pin a paper template to the wrong side of the remaining fabric in each pair and cut around the template, adding $^1/2''$ (1.2cm) seam allowance. Run a gathering thread around the edge of each fabric circle in the seam line, then draw up gathers so that the seam allowance turns over the paper template. Press, then remove template, baste to hold. Fold each circle in half along the horizontal grain line, then fold in half again along the vertical grain line, press. Open out circles.

Fold each of the 12 squares in half along the horizontal grain line, then fold in half again along the vertical grain line, press. Open out squares.

For each pair, place the wrong side of the circle on top of the right side of the square, matching fold lines. Pin in place then top-stitch around the circle, close to the folded edge, starting and stopping stitching on a centre fold line (**Diagram 4a**).

Cut along fold lines to make four quarter blocks, each containing a quarter circle (**Diagram 4b**). Trim fabric behind the quarter circle and trim the circle seam allowance, to $^1/4''$ (6mm).

Rearrange the 48 quarter blocks into groups of four, with a circle in the centre of each block, mixing the colours well but making sure the colours in each block complement each other. Join the quarter circles in each block to form 12 completed sugar bowl blocks.

Join the sugar bowl blocks to form four strips: two of two blocks and two of four blocks. With right sides together, join a two-block strip to either side of framed centre block, then join the four-block strips to top and bottom of the block (**Diagram 5**). Press seam allowances towards sugar bowl border.

The quilt top should now measure $40^1/_2''$ (103cm) square, including seam allowances.

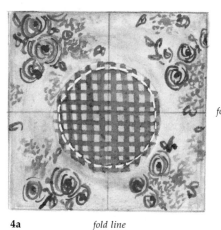

*fold line*

**4a**          *fold line*

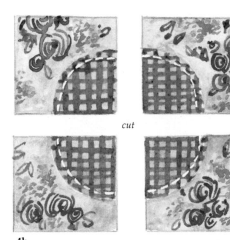

*cut*

**4b**

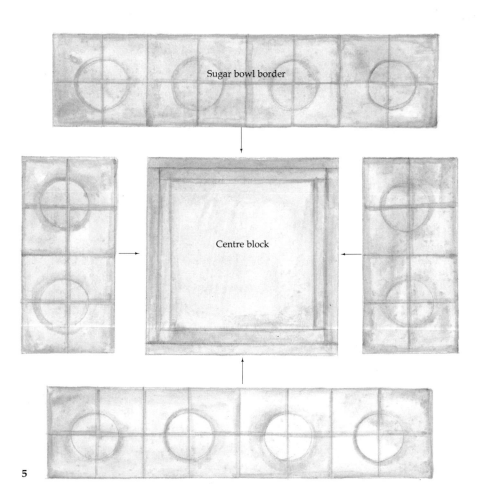

Sugar bowl border

Centre block

**5**

## Inner Border

**Note:** *Once again, measure the quilt top (through the centre) before cutting border strips. If the quilt is smaller than the measurement given, cut border strips a little wider to make up the difference.*

From red check fabric, cut two $2^1/_2$" x $40^1/_2$" (6.3cm x 103cm) strips, for side border strips, and two $2^1/_2$" x $44^1/_2$" (6.3cm x 113cm) strips, for top and bottom border strips.

With right sides together, join a side border strip to each side of quilt top. Have border strip uppermost when stitching so that it is easier to ease quilt top into size of border strip if necessary. Open out, and press seam allowances towards border strips.

Repeat to join longer top and bottom border strips, pressing seam allowances towards border.

The quilt top should now measure $44^1/_2$" (113cm) square, including seam allowances.

## Hourglass Border

From a mixture of light, medium and dark flannels, cut 48 squares, each $5^1/_4$" (13.3cm).

Organise squares into 24 complementary pairs, with each pair consisting of a darker and a lighter shade. Referring to diagrams and instructions for half-square triangles on page 115, join squares together to form 48 half-square triangle units.

Join half-square triangle units together, following instructions for quick-piecing quarter-square triangles on page 116, to form 48 quarter-square triangle units (hourglass blocks), each 4" (10cm) square.

Join hourglass blocks to form four strips: two of 11 blocks, and two of 13 blocks.

With right sides together and with hourglass border uppermost, stitch an 11-piece hourglass border strip to each side of quilt top. Once again, you may need to ease quilt into size of border strip, so have border strip uppermost when stitching.

Repeat to join the two 13-piece border strips to the top and bottom of the quilt. Press seam allowances towards inner border.

## Outer Border

From red check fabric, cut five $2^1/_2$" (6.3cm) strips across width of fabric. Join ends to make one long strip.

Measure length of quilt through centre of quilt top, and, from the pre-cut strip, cut two side border strips to this measurement. With right sides together and border strip uppermost, stitch a strip to either side of quilt top. Press seam allowances towards border strips.

Measure width of quilt through centre of quilt top, and, from remaining strip, cut two strips to this measurement. With right sides together, join these to top and bottom of quilt top. Press seam allowances towards outer border.

## Quilting

As the interest in this quilt lies in the mix of fabrics and patchwork patterning, the quilting has been kept to a minimum. It can be completed without marking.

Cut backing fabric piece in half across width of fabric to form two rectangles, each 65" x 45" (165cm x 115cm). With right sides together, stitch pieces together down long sides.

With backing seam centred horizontally across quilt, baste quilt top, batting and backing together, following directions for "Layering Quilt" on page 116.

Using brown perle cotton and following directions for "Hand Quilting" on page 117, outline quilt approximately $^1/_4$" (6mm) *inside* seam lines of the chimneys, roof, windows, door, lawn and outer frame. Outline quilt approximately $^1/_8$" (3mm) *outside* seam lines of the sugar bowl panel, inner border and outer border. Concentrate on achieving even stitches rather than tiny stitches.

## Binding

Following directions for "Straight Binding: Double" on page 118, cut strips from red flannel, join and apply to quilt edges.

Label and date your finished quilt.

Centre block

Inner frame

Outer frame

Sugar bowl panel

Inner border

Hourglass border

Outer border

A refreshingly lighthearted approach
that bypasses tradition in favour of
style, colour and expression ...

# Child's Button Quilt

*This distinctive button quilt displays a refreshing approach*

*to appliqué and quilting, one that bypasses tradition in favour of style, colour and expression.*

*Various plant and animal shapes have been rounded up and assembled on torn background blocks,*

*then outlined with delicate beading in a brilliant and quirky display.*

## MEASUREMENTS

Finished quilt measures approximately 110cm x 130cm (43$^1$/$_4$" x 51"), including prairie point border.

## MATERIALS

- 4.5m x 115cm (5yds x 45") cream homespun

- Small amount each of assorted cotton fabrics, in bright, solid colours, for appliqué shapes

- 120cm x 140cm (47" x 55") cotton batting

- 1m (1$^1$/$_4$yds) double-sided fusible webbing (such as Vliesofix)

- Stranded embroidery cotton, in 10 or 11 bright colours

- Cream machine thread

- Cream, navy blue and French blue perle cotton No. 8

- Small embroidery needle

- Quilting needles (betweens)

- Three packets 2mm glass seed beads (we used Mill Hill No. 00123)

- Assorted cream buttons (approximately 60)

## APPLIQUÉ OUTLINES

Before proceeding, read through "Super Quick Appliqué" instructions on page 114. All 30 appliqué outlines are printed full size on the pattern sheet and labelled with the letter C. Trace outlines for all shapes directly onto Vliesofix. Some shapes are used more than once — use the photograph on page 59, in which each shape is numbered, and the numbers on the pieces themselves as guides. Some shapes are made up of two or more overlapping pieces, each of which needs to be traced and cut separately. Trace around the broken lines and transfer the number on each shape to pieces that make up the shape; these numbers will assist you when reassembling the shapes on the background blocks.

Note that the shapes have been printed in reverse so that when they are applied to fabric they will be the right way round.

## CUTTING

There is no need to add seam allowances to appliqué outlines, as shapes are fused into place and raw edges covered by chain stitch. $1/4$" (6mm) seam allowance is **included** in other measurements.

From cream homespun, cut two rectangles, each $41^1/_4$" x 49" (105cm x 125cm), for quilt top and backing. Also cut or tear 30 squares, each $6^3/_4$" (17cm), for background blocks. From remaining homespun, cut approximately 100 squares, each $3^3/_4$" (9.5cm), for prairie point

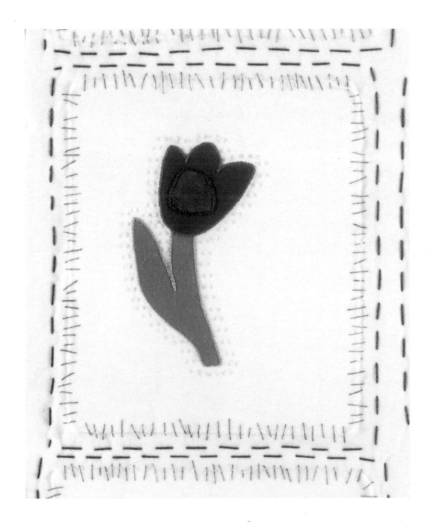

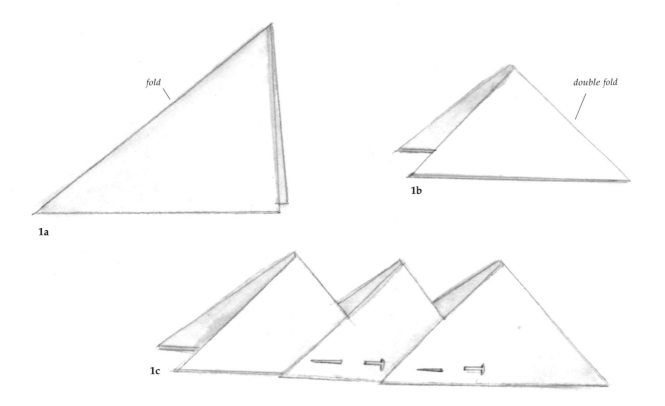

*fold*

**1a**

*double fold*

**1b**

**1c**

borders. Also cut five strips, each $6^1/_2$" x $6^3/_4$" (16.5cm x 17cm), for hanging loops.

From batting, cut a rectangle, $41^1/_4$" x 49" (105cm x 125cm).

## SEWING

### Appliqué and Embroidery

Fuse appliqué shapes into position on background blocks, using photograph on page 59 as a guide to placement and following "Super Quick Appliqué" instructions. Pay attention to the way in which pieces are layered to make up certain shapes; for example, the tops of the bird's legs are tucked slightly under the bird's body and the stem of the tulip is tucked under the flower. Refer back to the appliqué outlines, where concealed edges are indicated by broken lines.

Using two strands of embroidery cotton in desired colour and a small embroidery needle, work chain stitch (see page 119) around edge of each shape. The stitch must be right on the edge in order to cover both fabrics. The smaller the needle, the smaller the chain stitch will be.

### Assembling Quilt Top

Lay quilt top on a flat surface and position the 30 background blocks evenly on the fabric, with five blocks across and six blocks down. Leave approximately 1" (2.5cm) between each block, although you can vary the size of your quilt at this stage by adjusting the distance between blocks. When satisfied with the layout, pin then baste blocks in position.

Using one strand of embroidery cotton in chosen colour and referring to photograph on page 56, work a primitive overstitch around each block. There is no need to turn under the raw edges, and the more uneven your stitches, the better the result.

### Prairie Point Border

Fold each border square in half diagonally (**Diagram 1a**) and press, then fold in half again and press (**Diagram 1b**). We used 35 triangles for each side border and 27 for the lower border. Slip one triangle into the pocket of the next triangle to the halfway point, and pin (**Diagram 1c**). Continue in this manner until you have required number of prairie points for each border.

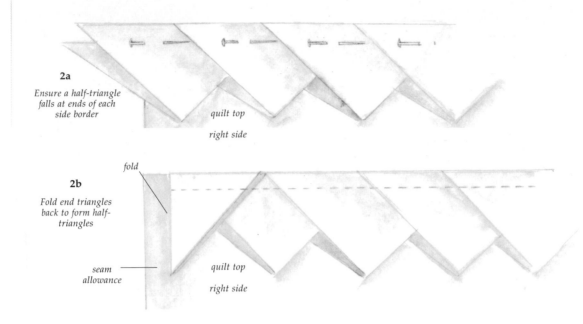

**2a**

*Ensure a half-triangle falls at ends of each side border*

quilt top

right side

**2b**

*fold*

*Fold end triangles back to form half-triangles*

*seam allowance*

quilt top

right side

With right sides together and raw edges even, pin the bottom border to the bottom edge of the quilt top, adjusting length of border if necessary and making sure a complete triangle falls at each end (allow for $^1/_4$", or 6mm, seam allowance). Baste, then stitch in place.

Pin the side borders in place, right sides together and raw edges even, this time ensuring that half a triangle falls at each end (**Diagram 2a**). Fold the end triangles back under to form half triangles, baste, then stitch side borders in position (**Diagram 2a**). Open out borders, and press.

### Hanging Loops

Fold hanging loop strips in half lengthwise, and stitch long side. Turn each loop through to right side, press and fold in half crosswise. With right sides together and raw edges even, position hanging loops along top edge of quilt top; align the outer two loops with side edges and place remaining loops at approximately 6" (15cm) intervals. Stitch in position.

### Quilting

There is no traditional quilting in this quilt; the beading around the shapes and the running stitch around the squares keep the layers together.

Mark an outline around each appliquéd shape, approximately $^1/_4$" (6mm) from edge, using a soft lead pencil.

Following instructions for "Layering Quilt" on page 116, baste quilt top, batting and backing together.

Using a neat running stitch and cream perle cotton, sew an outline of small glass beads around each shape, following markings, with beads about $^1/_4$" (6mm) apart. Be sure to take the needle through three layers of fabric to secure each square.

Using navy perle cotton, work large, irregular running stitches just outside the edges of each of the 30 squares. Using French blue perle cotton, work a row of irregular running stitch around the outside edge of the quilt.

### Binding and Finishing

The quilt can be completed with a modified folded finish (see page 118). After folding the raw edges of the backing over to enclose the batting, slip-stitch this folded edge over the border seam line.

To finish, sew on the 60 buttons in a line along the top of the quilt.

Sign and date your finished quilt, and hang on a decorative rod, if desired.

Cot Quilt

# MINIS
*and*
# Lap Quilts

The mini and lap-sized quilts

showcased here offer all the challenges

of larger quilts, yet won't take a

lifetime to complete — they also

encourage you to experiment with

design and technique. The bowtie quilt

introduces foundation piecing, while

the crazy patchwork quilt and garden

sampler involve colour and pattern

mixing. The cot quilt is included just

because it's irresistible.

For ease of piecing, a stylised
"crazy" quilt that contains
a repeating block ...

# Crazy Patchwork Quilt

*"Crazy" patchwork was particularly popular in Victorian times, favoured for its*

*highly decorative effects created from the tiniest scraps of fabric. Typically pieced from silks and*

*velvets, crazy quilts were more aesthetic than functional — they were used to embellish a bed rather*

*than keep the occupant warm, if they were placed on a bed at all. Our crazy quilt is serviceable and*

*attractive, being made of warm and washable flannels. For ease of piecing it contains a repeating block,*

*with the haphazard use of fabrics suggesting randomness.*

## MEASUREMENTS

Finished quilt measures approximately 123cm x 154cm ($48^1/_2$" x $60^1/_2$").

## MATERIALS

- Approximately 25 assorted light, medium and dark printed and plain flannels: 4.5m x 115cm (5yds x 45") in total

- 130cm x 160cm (51" x 63") batting or flannel

- 2.7m x 115cm (3yds x 45") printed flannel, for backing

- 0.5m x 115cm ($^2/_3$yd x 45") plain flannel, for binding

- Coordinating machine thread

- Quilting thread

- Perle cotton No. 8 in five contrasting colours

- Quilting needles (betweens)

## TEMPLATES

While appearing to consist of an all-over pattern of randomly placed patches, this quilt is made up of repeating blocks. Each block consists of eight patches but only five different shapes (A, B, C, X, Y and Z), with three of these shapes being irregular and cut from templates. Templates for shapes X, Y and Z are printed on the pattern sheet and marked with the letter D. Referring to "Making Templates" on page 114, make a template each of X, Y and Z.

## CUTTING

**Note:** *¹/₄″ (6mm) seam allowance is **included** on templates and in all given measurements.*

Refer to **Diagram 1** and the accompanying key when cutting patches for the blocks. From assorted light, medium and dark flannels, cut 20 each of X, Y, Z and B shapes, and 40 each of A and C shapes.

**KEY:**
A = 4¹/₂″ x 4″ (11.4cm x 10cm)
B = 4¹/₂″ x 6¹/₄″ (11.4cm x 15.8cm)
C = 6¹/₂″ x 3¹/₄″ (16.5cm x 8.2cm)

X = template shape
Y = template shape
Z = template shape

## SEWING

### Piecing Blocks

Following the layout for each block shown in **Diagram 1**, arrange patches into 20 blocks, making sure the tonal pattern pleases you.

For each block, stitch patches together in following sequence, referring to **Diagrams 1 and 2**: Stitch X to A, and press seam allowances towards A. Stitch Y to X/A, press seams towards Y. Stitch Z to X/Y, press seams towards Z. Stitch A to B, press seams towards A. Stitch A/B to Z/X/A, press seams towards Z/X/A. Stitch C to C, pressing seams to the left-hand side. Stitch C/C to A/Z, pressing seams towards A/Z.

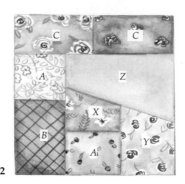

Finished block

### Assembling Quilt Top

Lay out completed blocks in four rows of five, turning blocks so that you get a good mix of fabrics. With right sides together, stitch blocks together in sequence, one row at a time. Stitch rows together, aligning seams. Press assembled quilt top.

### Quilting

There is no need to mark quilting pattern before quilting.

Cut backing fabric in half across width of fabric to form two 54″ (135cm) lengths. With right sides together, stitch lengths together along 54″ edge. Press seam allowances to one side. Following directions for "Layering Quilt" on page 116, baste quilt top, batting or flannel, and backing together.

Referring to "Quilting" on page 117, machine quilt in-the-ditch between each block, then, using perle cotton in contrasting colours, outline quilt by hand approximately ¹/₂″ (1.2cm) from the edge of each shape.

### Binding

Following instructions for "Straight Binding: Double" on page 118, cut strips from binding fabric, join and apply to quilt edges.

Label and sign your completed quilt.

The blocks are made using quick-piecing
methods, so the quilt top is surprisingly
easy to assemble ...

# Garden Sampler Quilt

*Each of the blocks in this sampler quilt displays a unique combination of half-square triangles and flying geese, giving you a chance to experiment with different fabric mixes. The blocks can be made using quick-piecing methods, so the quilt top is surprisingly easy to assemble. And the result will be no less impressive if you simplify the quilting design, as most of the interest lies in the patchwork patterning. It's the ideal project for the impatient patchworker!*

## MEASUREMENTS

Finished quilt measures approximately 115cm x 145cm (45" x 57").

## MATERIALS

- 0.5m x 120cm (²/₃yd x 47") calico, for background in pieced blocks (Fabric A)

- 0.2m x 115cm (¹/₄yd x 45") each of 18 medium and dark printed coordinating fabrics (Fabrics B–S)

- 1m x 115cm (1¹/₄yds x 45") printed fabric, for setting squares and triangles (Fabric T)

- 0.3m x 115cm (¹/₃yd x 45") spotted fabric, for inner border (Fabric U)

- 1.5m x 115cm (1²/₃yds x 45") floral fabric, for outer border (Fabric V)

- 2.5m x 115cm (2³/₄yds x 45") fabric, for backing (Fabric W)

- 0.3m x 115cm (¹/₃yd x 45") striped fabric, for binding (Fabric X)

- 130cm x 160cm (51" x 63") cotton batting

- Coordinating machine thread

- Quilting thread

- Quilting needles (betweens)

## SEWING

### Pieced Blocks

The pieced blocks consist of varying arrangements of squares, half-square triangle units and flying geese units. Before proceeding, refer to the diagrams and instructions for quick-piecing half-square triangle and flying geese units on page 115.

For the blocks you will need a mixture of calico (Fabric A), and medium and dark printed fabrics (Fabrics B–S). Refer to the photograph on page 71 when selecting fabrics. For half-square triangle units, cut required number of squares, then sort them into correct pairs according to the combinations given for each block. Once all the units for each block are completed, piece them in the arrangement shown in the diagram accompanying the instructions for the block.

The small half-square triangle units measure 2″ (5cm) square, the flying geese units measure 2″ x 4″ (5cm x 10cm) and each pieced block measures 8″ (20.2cm) square.

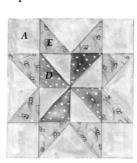

**Block 1:** From Fabric A, cut eight squares, each $2^7/8''$ (7.3cm), from Fabric B, cut four squares, each $2^7/8''$, and from Fabric C, cut four squares, each $2^7/8''$, for half-square triangles.

Join four Fabric A squares to four Fabric B squares, and join four Fabric A squares to four Fabric C squares, to form 16 half-square triangles in total.

Referring to **Diagram 1**, join units to form the complete block.

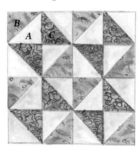

**Block 2:** From Fabric A, cut two squares, each $2^7/8''$ (7.3cm), and from Fabric D, cut two squares, each $2^7/8''$, for half-square triangles. From Fabric A, cut four rectangles, each $2^1/2''$ x $4^1/2''$ (6.3cm x 11.4cm), and from Fabric E, cut eight squares, each $2^1/2''$, for flying geese units. From Fabric A, cut four squares, each $2^1/2''$, for corners.

Join two Fabric A squares to two Fabric D squares, to form four half-square triangles. Join each Fabric A rectangle to two Fabric E squares, to form four flying geese units in total.

Referring to **Diagram 2**, join units to form the complete block.

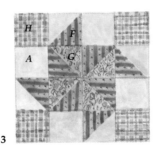

**Block 3:** From Fabric A, cut two squares, each $2^7/8''$ (7.3cm), from Fabric F, cut four squares, each $2^7/8''$, and from Fabric G, cut two squares, each $2^7/8''$, for half-square triangles. From Fabric A, cut four squares, each $2^1/2''$ (6.3cm), for piecing squares. From Fabric H, cut four squares, each $2^1/2''$, for corners.

Join two Fabric A squares to two Fabric F squares, to form four half-square triangles. Join two Fabric G squares to remaining two Fabric F squares, to form another four half-square triangles.

Referring to **Diagram 3**, join units to form the complete block.

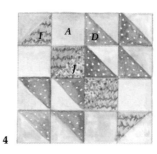

**Block 4:** From Fabric A, cut five squares, each $2^7/8''$ (7.3cm), from Fabric D, cut four squares, each $2^7/8''$, from Fabric I, cut two squares, each $2^7/8''$, and from Fabric J, cut one $2^7/8''$ square, for half-square triangles. From Fabric A, also cut four squares, each $2^1/2''$ (6.3cm), for piecing squares.

Join four Fabric A squares to four Fabric D squares, one Fabric A square to one Fabric I square, and one Fabric I square to one Fabric J square, to form 12 half-square triangles in total.

Referring to **Diagram 4**, join units to form the complete block.

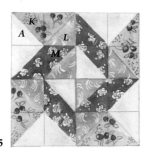

**Block 5:** From Fabric A, cut five squares, each $2^7/_8''$ (7.3cm), from Fabric K, cut four squares, each $2^7/_8''$, from Fabric L, cut three squares, each $2^7/_8''$, and from Fabric M, cut four squares, each $2^7/_8''$, for half-square triangles.

Join two Fabric A squares to two Fabric K squares, three Fabric A squares to three Fabric M squares, two Fabric K squares to two Fabric L squares, and one Fabric L square to one Fabric M square, to form 16 half-square triangles in total.

Referring to **Diagram 5**, join units to form the complete block.

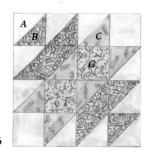

**Block 6:** From Fabric A, cut five squares, each $2^7/_8''$ (7.3cm), from Fabric B, cut four squares, each $2^7/_8''$, and from Fabric C, cut three squares, each $2^7/_8''$, for half-square triangles. From Fabric A, cut two squares, each $2^1/_2''$ (6.3cm), for two corners. From Fabric G, cut two squares, each $2^1/_2''$, for centre squares.

Join three Fabric A squares to three Fabric B squares, two Fabric A squares to two Fabric C squares, and one Fabric B square to one Fabric C square, to form 12 half-square triangles in total.

Referring to **Diagram 6**, join units to form the complete block.

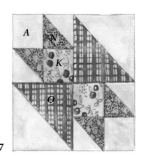

**Block 7:** From Fabric A, cut two squares, each $2^7/_8''$ (7.3cm), and from Fabric N, cut two squares, each $2^7/_8''$, for half-square triangles. From Fabric A, cut one $4^7/_8''$ (12.3cm) square,

and from Fabric O, cut one $4^7/_8''$ square, for large half-square triangles. From Fabric K, cut two squares, each $2^1/_2''$ (6.3cm), for piecing squares. From Fabric A, cut two squares, each $2^1/_2''$, for two corners.

Join two Fabric A squares to two Fabric N squares, to form four half-square triangles. Also join large Fabric A square to large Fabric O square, to form two large half-square triangles.

Referring to **Diagram 7**, join units to form the complete block.

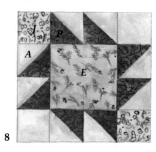

**Block 8:** From Fabric A, cut four squares, each $2^7/_8''$ (7.3cm), and from Fabric P, cut four squares, each $2^7/_8''$, for half-square triangles. From Fabric A, cut two squares, each $2^1/_2''$ (6.3cm), and from Fabric J, cut two squares, each $2^1/_2''$, for corner squares. From Fabric E, cut one $4^1/_2''$ (11.4cm) square, for centre.

Join four Fabric A squares to four Fabric P squares, to form eight half-square triangles.

Referring to **Diagram 8**, join units to form the complete block.

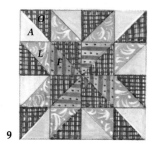

**Block 9:** From Fabric A, cut four squares, each $2^7/_8''$ (7.3cm), from Fabric F, cut two squares, each $2^7/_8''$, from Fabric L, cut four squares, each $2^7/_8''$, and from Fabric O, cut six squares, each $2^7/_8''$, for half-square triangles.

Join two Fabric A squares to two Fabric O squares, two Fabric A squares to two Fabric L squares, two Fabric L squares to two Fabric O squares, and two Fabric F squares to two Fabric O squares, to form 16 half-square triangles in total.

Referring to **Diagram 9**, join units to form the complete block.

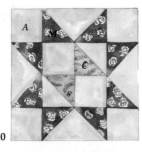

**10**

**Block 10:** From Fabric A, cut one $2^7/8''$ (7.3cm) square, and from Fabric C, cut one $2^7/8''$ square, for half-square triangles. From Fabric A, cut six squares, each $2^1/2''$ (6.3cm), for corners and piecing squares. From Fabric A, cut also four rectangles, each $2^1/2'' \times 4^1/2''$ (6.3cm x 11.4cm), and from Fabric M, cut eight squares, each $2^1/2''$ (6.3cm), for flying geese units.

Join Fabric A square to Fabric C square to form two half-square triangles. Join two Fabric M squares to each Fabric A rectangle, to form four flying geese units in total.

Referring to **Diagram 10**, join units to form the complete block.

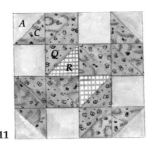

**11**

**Block 11:** From Fabric A, cut two squares, each $2^7/8''$ (7.3cm), from Fabric C, cut five squares, each $2^7/8''$, from Fabric Q, cut four squares, each $2^7/8''$, and from Fabric R, cut one $2^7/8''$ square, for half-square triangles. From Fabric A, cut also four squares, each $2^1/2''$ (6.3cm), for piecing squares.

Join two Fabric A squares to two Fabric C squares, three Fabric C squares to three Fabric Q squares, and one Fabric Q square to one Fabric R square.

Referring to **Diagram 11**, join units to form the complete block.

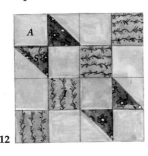

**12**

**Block 12:** From Fabric A, cut two squares, each $2^7/8''$ (7.3cm), and from Fabric S, cut two squares, each $2^7/8''$, for half-square triangles. From Fabric A, cut eight squares, each $2^1/2''$ (6.3cm), and from Fabric I, cut four squares, each $2^1/2''$, for piecing squares.

Join two Fabric A squares to two Fabric S squares, to form four half-square triangles.

Referring to **Diagram 12**, join units to form the complete block.

### Assembling Quilt Top

As the blocks are set on point, you will need to add setting blocks between the pieced blocks and complete the outer edges and each corner of the quilt with appropriate setting triangles.

From Fabric T, cut six squares, each $8^1/2''$ (21.5cm), for setting blocks. Cut three squares, each $12^5/8''$ (32cm), then cut each square diagonally twice, to give 12 triangles (there will be two spares) with the straight grain running along the long side of each triangle, for setting triangles. Also cut two squares, each $6^1/2''$ (16.5cm), then cut each square diagonally once, for small corner setting triangles.

Referring to **Diagram 13**, and with right sides facing, join blocks and setting triangles together to form rows. Press seams away from pieced blocks. Stitch rows together, beginning at top right-hand corner. Stitch two remaining small setting triangles to outer edges of Block 3 and Block 10.

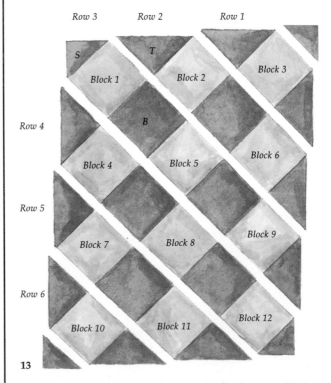

**13**

T = setting triangle   S = small setting triangle   B = setting block

## Borders

**Inner border:** From Fabric U, cut five 1¼" (3cm) strips across width of fabric. Join strips using diagonal seams (see **Diagram 13a** in "Straight Binding: Double" on page 118). Measure length of quilt through centre of quilt top, then cut two strips from joined strip to length measurement, for side border strips. With right sides together and border strip uppermost, stitch a strip to each side of quilt top. Open out and press seams towards border strip.

Repeat this process, measuring width of quilt after joining side border strips and cutting strips from remainder of joined strip, to join top and bottom border strips.

**Outer border:** From Fabric V, cut four 6" (15.2cm) strips along length of fabric. Measure length of quilt through centre of quilt top and trim two strips to this measurement, for side border strips. With right sides together, join a side border strip to each side of quilt.

Measure width of quilt through centre of quilt top, trim remaining two strips to this measurement, and join to top and bottom of quilt.

## Quilting

Referring to "Marking Quilting Patterns" on page 116, mark quilting lines on quilt top. You can follow our quilting design or quilt as desired. Our quilt was outline quilted around all pieces, with a heart variation in each corner triangle, a feather and heart design in each setting triangle, a flower and feather medallion in each setting block (all printed on pattern sheet) and overlapping rainbows in the outer border (use Lemoyne Star Quilt border quilting pattern on the pattern sheet).

Cut backing fabric in half lengthwise and stitch lengths together along 49" (125cm) edge. Press seam to one side. Baste quilt top, batting and backing together, following instructions in "Layering Quilt" on page 116.

Referring to "Hand Quilting" on page 117, quilt along marked lines.

## Binding

Following directions for "Straight Binding: Double" on page 118, cut 2⅛" (5.3cm) strips from binding fabric, join and apply to quilt edges,

Label and date your finished quilt.

*Traditionally, miniature quilts like this one were used to cover dolls' cots ...*

# Mini Bowtie

*Traditionally, miniature quilts like this one were used to cover dolls' cots.*

*But if your doll doesn't mind sharing, this lovely little quilt would also make*

*an attractive wall-hanging or table runner.*

## MEASUREMENTS

Finished quilt measures approximately 37cm x 44.5cm ($14^1/2$" x $17^1/2$").

## MATERIALS

- 20cm x 25cm (8" x 10") each of 12 assorted medium and dark fabrics, and at least 10 assorted light fabrics, for bowties, backgrounds and pieced border

- 0.2m x 115cm ($^1/4$yd x 45") light fabric, for inner border

- 0.2m x 115cm ($^1/4$yd x 45") dark fabric, for binding

- 50cm x 60cm (20" x 24") printed fabric, for backing

- 50cm x 60cm (20" x 24") cotton batting

- 1m x 115cm ($1^1/4$yds x 45") transparent material, such as lightweight interfacing or tracing paper, for foundation patterns

- Coordinating machine thread

- Quilting thread

- Quilting needles (betweens)

## FOUNDATION PATTERNS

Each bowtie block consists of two pieced half blocks. These half blocks are identical when pieced, but rotated when joined to make the complete block. The quilt centre is made up of 12 bowtie blocks, a total of 24 separate half blocks. Each of the four pieced borders consists of eight squares, with each square comprising two triangles.

Foundation patterns for the half bowtie block and the two pieced borders are printed on the pattern sheet. Trace onto foundation material. You will need 24 foundation patterns for the bowtie blocks and two each of the two foundation patterns for the borders. Transfer numbers to each foundation pattern — these refer to the order in which you stitch the patches and also indicate the right side of the foundation pattern.

## CUTTING

**Note:** $^1/_4''$ *(6mm) seam allowance is* **included** *on foundation patterns and in all measurements.*

From a mixture of light fabrics, cut 24 squares, each approximately $2^1/_2''$ (6.3cm), cutting two squares from same fabric for each block, for bowtie backgrounds. Sort into piles of same-fabric squares.

From a mixture of medium and dark fabrics, cut 24 squares, each approximately $2^1/_2''$ (6.3cm), and 24 triangles, each with longest side approximately $3^1/_2''$ (8.8cm), cutting two squares and two triangles from same fabric for each block, for bowties. Sort into piles of same-fabric squares and triangles.

From a mixture of light, medium and dark fabrics, cut 32 squares, each approximately 3" (7.5cm), for pieced border. Cut each square diagonally once to make 64 triangles. Sort triangles into light, medium and dark piles.

## SEWING

When piecing the blocks, place the fabric patches, right sides together, on *wrong side* of foundation pattern. Then, using a small stitch length, follow the stitching line on *right side* of foundation pattern, which is the side on which the numbers and stitching lines are marked.

## Bowtie Blocks

**Making half blocks:** Place bowtie background square (light fabric) on a flat surface, wrong side up. Position bowtie foundation pattern, right side up, so that 1 is centred on top of fabric square (**Diagram 1**). Pin to secure.

Fold foundation pattern back on sewing line between 1 and 2, trim seam allowance to $^1/_4''$ (6mm) (**Diagram 2**).

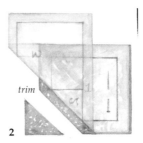

Turn foundation pattern over and, with right sides together and raw edges even, place dark bowtie triangle on light background square (**Diagram 3**).

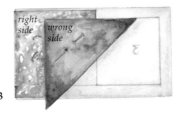

Turn foundation pattern over again so that it is right side up, pin to secure. Stitch on line between 1 and 2, continuing several stitches either end of line (**Diagram 4**).

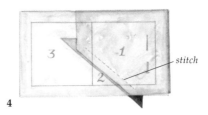

There is no need to back-stitch, as intersecting lines of stitches will secure stitching. Open out triangle, finger press seams towards triangle.

Fold foundation pattern back on stitching line between 1, 2 and 3 and trim seam allowance to $^1/_4$" (6mm) (**Diagram 5**).

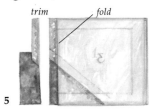

Turn foundation pattern over and, with right sides together and raw edges even, place dark bowtie square on completed square. Turn foundation pattern over so that it is right side up, pin to secure. Stitch on line between 1, 2 and 3 (**Diagram 6**), continuing several stitches either side of line. Open out square, finger press seams towards darker fabric. Trim outer seam allowances to $^1/_4$" (6mm).

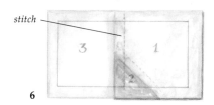

You have now completed one half bowtie block (**Diagram 7**). Repeat this procedure for second half bowtie block, using same light and dark fabrics. Make 12 matching pairs of half blocks.

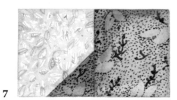

Finished half bowtie block

**Piecing half blocks:** With right sides facing, dark squares in opposite corners and dark centres together, pin matched pairs together, then chain piece (see "Piecing Fabrics" on page 115) to form completed blocks (**Diagram 8**). Press seam allowances open. Repeat until you have 12 complete blocks. Trim all blocks to $3^1/_2$" (8.8cm) square.

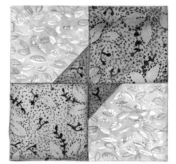

Finished bowtie block

## Assembling Quilt Centre

Arrange completed bowtie blocks into four rows of three, using photograph on page 77 as a guide. With right sides together, join blocks to form rows, then join rows to form quilt centre. The quilt centre should measure $12^1/_2$" x $9^1/_2$" (31.8cm x 24cm), including seam allowances. If the quilt is smaller than the measurements given, cut border strips a little wider to make up the difference.

## Borders

**Inner border:** Measure length of quilt top through centre of quilt. From inner border fabric, cut two strips, each $1^1/_2$" (3.7cm) wide, to this measurement. With right sides together and border strip uppermost, join a strip to each long side of quilt top. Press seams towards border strips. Repeat this process to join top and bottom border strips, measuring width of quilt top through centre of quilt.

**Outer (pieced) border:** When placing fabrics in position for border, ensure that you have a good contrasting mix of light, medium and dark.

Place light triangle, wrong side up, on a flat surface. Position one foundation border pattern, right side up, so that 1 is centred on top of triangle (**Diagram 9**). Pin to secure.

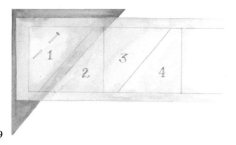

Fold foundation pattern back on the stitching line between 1 and 2, and trim seam allowance to $1/4$" (6mm) (**Diagram 10**).

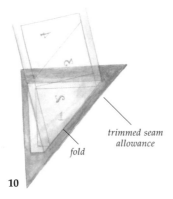

trimmed seam
allowance

fold

**10**

Turn foundation pattern over and, with right sides together and raw edges even, place dark triangle on light triangle. Turn foundation pattern over again so that it is right side up, pin to secure. Stitch on line between 1 and 2, continuing several stitches either side of the line (**Diagram 11**). Open out triangle and finger press seam allowances towards darker fabric.

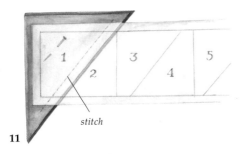

stitch

**11**

Fold foundation pattern back on the stitching line between 2 and 3, and trim seam allowance to $1/4$" (6mm) (**Diagram 12**).

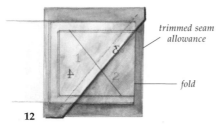

trimmed seam
allowance

fold

**12**

Turn foundation pattern over and, with right sides together and raw edges even, position another light triangle on stitched dark triangle (**Diagram 13**).

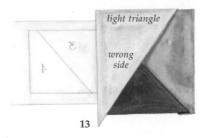

light triangle

wrong
side

**13**

Turn over again so that foundation paper is right side up, pin to secure. Stitch on line between 2 and 3. Open out triangle and finger press seam allowances towards darker fabric (**Diagram 14**).

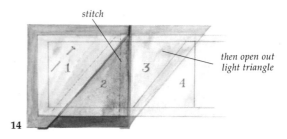

stitch

then open out
light triangle

**14**

Repeat until end of the border foundation pattern is reached. Stitch along outline of border pattern, then trim seam allowance to $1/4$" (6mm).

Make another border using same pattern, and two more using remaining border pattern.

With right sides together, join a pieced side border strip to each side of quilt top, press seams towards border strips. Then join top and bottom border strips, pressing seams towards strips.

## Quilting

Remove all foundation patterns from fabric.

Referring to "Layering Quilt" on page 116, baste quilt top, batting and backing together.

Referring to "Quilting" on page 117, quilt as desired. The pieced triangles in the border of our quilt have been quilted in-the-ditch, while the bowtie backgrounds have been outline quilted $1/4$" (6mm) from the seams.

## Binding

Referring to "Straight Binding: Double" on page 118, cut strips from binding fabric, join and apply to quilt edge.

Label and date your finished quilt.

Continuing a timeworn
tradition of handmaking
gifts for the newborn ...

# Cot Quilt

*This diminutive quilt was sewn for the maker's grandchildren,*

*continuing a timeworn tradition of handmaking gifts for the newborn.*

*It's certainly tiny enough to be created by hand, but it will look just as good*

*if it is machine pieced. Whichever method you choose, you'll have the satisfaction of*

*creating a lasting gift or addition to a nursery.*

## MEASUREMENTS

Finished quilt measures approximately 58.5cm x 73.5cm (23" x 29").

## MATERIALS

- 18 assorted light, dark and medium yellow and blue prints, each at least 12cm x 20cm (5" x 8"), for four-patch blocks

- 0.2m x 115cm ($^1/_4$yd x 45") very light floral print, for setting blocks

- 0.2m x 115cm ($^1/_4$yd x 45") yellow check, for border

- 66cm x 81cm (26" x 32") yellow floral print, for backing

- 0.2m x 115cm ($^1/_4$yd x 45") blue floral print, for binding

- 66cm x 81cm (26" x 32") lightweight batting

- Coordinating machine thread

- Embroidery needle (if hand piecing)

- Quilting thread

- Quilting needles (betweens)

## SEWING

**Note:** $^1/_4$″ *(6mm) seam allowance is **included** in given measurements.*

### Blocks

Our quilt is made up of two different types of four-patch blocks — Block 1 and Block 2, as shown in **Diagram 2** — alternating with setting blocks.

If you wish to hand-piece the quilt, from the 18 assorted fabrics, cut a total of 216 squares, each $1^1/_2$″ (3.7cm).

Referring to "Hand piecing" on page 115, join squares together to make Blocks 1 and 2. You will need 54 blocks in total.

If you wish to machine-piece your quilt, from each of the 18 assorted fabrics, cut three strips, each $1^1/_2$″ x 7″ (3.7cm x 17.8cm).

With right sides facing, stitch two contrasting strips together. Open out strips, press seams towards darker fabric. Continue to stitch contrasting strips together; you will have 27 stitched strips in total. Cut stitched strips across into $1^1/_2$″ (3.7cm) segments; you will have 108 segments in total.

Arrange these segments into groups of two, using segments from the same stitched strip for Block 1 (**Diagram 1a**) and segments from different stitched strips for Block 2 (**Diagram 1b**). With right sides together and matching seams, stitch segments together, to form 54 four-patch blocks.

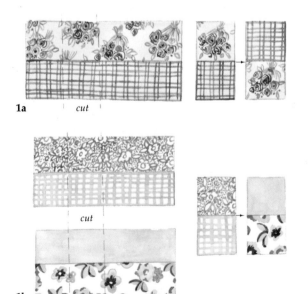

**1a**      cut

**1b**      cut

**2**     Finished Block 1          Finished Block 2

### Assembling Quilt Top

From very light floral print, cut 54 squares, each $2^1/_2$″ (6.3cm), for setting blocks.

Alternating four-patch blocks and setting blocks, lay out blocks in 12 rows of nine, and rearrange until you are satisfied with the tonal pattern. With right sides facing, stitch blocks together to form rows, pressing seams away from four-patch blocks. Stitch rows together, aligning seams.

### Border

Measure length of quilt through centre of quilt top. From border fabric, cut $2^3/_4$″ (7cm) strips to this measurement, for side border strips. With right sides together, stitch a side border strip to each side of quilt top. Have border strip uppermost when stitching so that you can ease quilt into size of border strip if necessary. Open out, and press seam allowances towards border strips.

Repeat this process to cut and join top and bottom border strips, measuring width of quilt after side border strips have been joined.

### Quilting

There is no need to mark quilting lines on quilt top, as our quilt is simply outline quilted $^1/_8$″ (3mm) *inside* the seam lines of the setting blocks, with the lines extended into the border.

Baste quilt top, batting and backing together, following directions in "Layering Quilt" on page 116.

Hand quilt as desired.

### Binding

Referring to "Straight Binding: Double" on page 118, cut $2^1/_2$″ (6.3cm) strips from binding fabric, join and apply to edges of quilt.

Label and date your finished quilt.

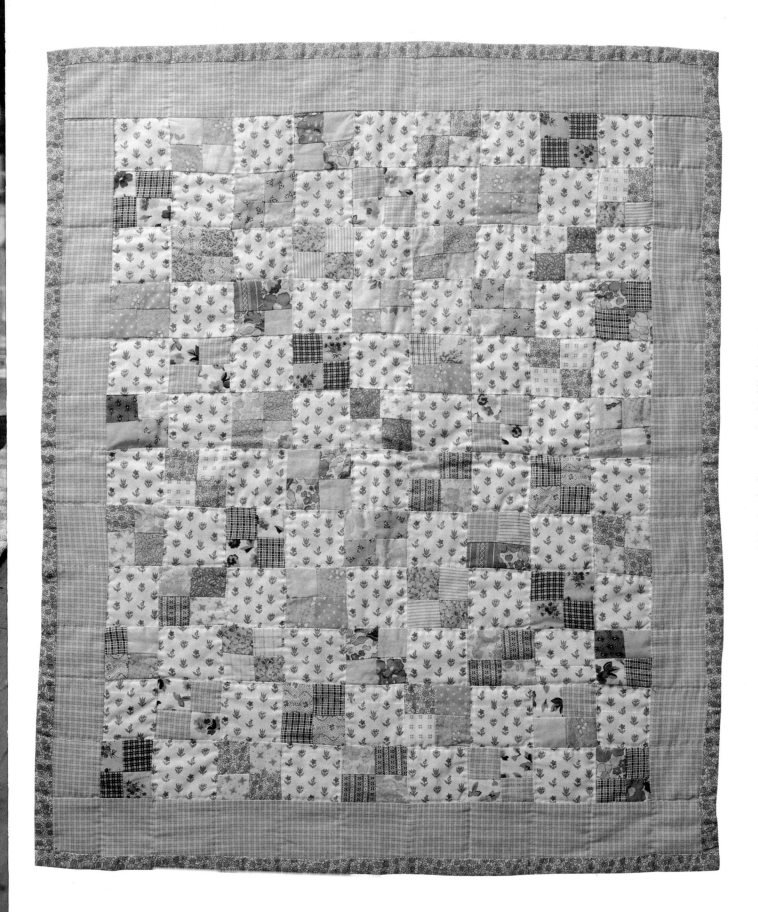

*With its spring garden charm, this cloth provides the perfect backdrop for warm weather eating ...*

# Floral
# Tablecloth

*With its spring garden charm, this cloth provides the perfect backdrop*

*for warm weather eating. You'll probably want to bring it out regardless of the season,*

*to enjoy its floral exuberance all year round.*

## MEASUREMENTS

Finished cloth measures approximately 130cm (51") square.

## MATERIALS

- Dark, medium and light floral fabrics (see **Note**, below)

- 0.2m x 115cm ($^1$/₄yd x 45") plain écru fabric

- 1.5m x 150cm (1$^2$/₃ yds x 59") floral fabric, for backing and binding

- Template plastic or cardboard (optional)

- Coordinating machine thread

**Note:** *Three different floral designs are included — one densely patterned with flowers, one patterned with fewer flowers on a light background, and one with just a few sprigs on a light background. You do not have to use three different fabrics; a piece of floral fabric that has quite heavily printed areas on a more sparsely sprigged background might serve for all three floral designs, or at least two of them. If you use the same fabric for all three designs, you will need 2.5–3m (2$^3$/₄–3$^1$/₃yds), allowing for wastage where the pattern is not usable. If you do choose to use three different fabrics, make sure that they tone in with each other. You will need approximately 0.8m x 115cm (1yd x 45") each of the dark floral and medium floral fabrics, plus approximately 0.5m ($^2$/₃yd) of the lightly sprigged fabric.*

## CUTTING

Using the layout diagram as a guide, cut required number of $3^3/8''$ (8.5cm) squares, making a template or using a rotary cutter and ruler. $^1/_4''$ (6mm) seam allowance is **included** in all measurements.

Arrange your fabrics into four separate piles as you cut, ranging from dark to light.

From dark floral fabric, cut 105 squares.

From medium floral fabric, cut 104 squares.

From light floral fabric, cut 64 squares.

From plain écru fabric, cut 16 squares.

From floral fabric, cut one 50" (127cm) square, for backing.

## SEWING

### *Assembling Cloth Top*

Arrange fabric squares into rows, following layout diagram below. Beginning with top row, and with right sides facing, stitch squares together in sequence to form rows. Press seam allowances open.

With right sides facing, stitch rows together, aligning seams, until patchwork top is complete. Press seam allowances open.

### *Backing and Binding*

Place backing wrong side up on a flat surface and place patchwork on top, right side up. Baste the outer edges together to hold, and trim backing.

Measure length of cloth through centre. From floral fabric, cut two $2^1/_8''$ (5.3cm) strips to this measurement, for side binding strips. With right sides together and raw edges even, stitch strips to each side of cloth. Have binding strip uppermost when stitching so that you can ease cloth into size of strip if necessary. Press under seam allowance on remaining raw edges of binding, fold binding to wrong side of cloth and slip-stitch pressed edges of binding in place over seam.

Repeat process to cut and join top and bottom binding strips, measuring width of cloth after joining side binding strips. Fold in raw edges neatly at each corner before slip-stitching to backing.

Dark floral fabric

Medium floral fabric

Light floral fabric

Plain écru fabric

Layout diagram

# Heart
# Table Runner

# Heart Table Runner

❖

*With its classic simplicity of shape, the heart motif is a natural candidate for the decorative arts.*

*And, with its many positive connotations, it is not surprising that this symbol is a favourite*

*with craftspeople. Here it has been appliquéd onto a table runner, warmly coloured in the*

*country tradition, to provide a pretty and practical alternative to a tablecloth.*

## MEASUREMENTS

Finished runner measures 38cm x 150cm (15" x 59").

## MATERIALS

- 10cm (4") square each of 10 different printed cottons in coordinating colours, for appliquéd hearts

- 15cm (6") square each of 20 different cotton fabrics in coordinating and contrasting colours, for background squares

- 0.3m x 115cm ($^1/_3$yd x 45") coordinating cotton fabric, for border

- 0.8m x 115cm (1yd x 45") contrasting cotton fabric, for backing

- 0.4m x 150cm ($^1/_2$yd x 59") batting

- Coordinating machine thread

- Contrasting quilting thread

- Quilting needles (betweens)

- 24 buttons in assorted sizes and shades of a selected colour

## APPLIQUÉ OUTLINE

Before proceeding, read through "Traditional Appliqué Method 1" on page 114. The heart outline is printed full size on this page. Trace onto paper 10 times.

## CUTTING

When cutting hearts, remember to **add** $^1/_4$" (6mm) seam allowance all round. $^1/_4$" (6mm) seam allowance is **included** in all other measurements.

From each of the 10 appliqué fabrics, cut one heart.

From backing fabric, cut two rectangles, each 20" x 31$^1/_2$" (51cm x 80cm).

## SEWING

### Appliqué and Piecing

Centre a heart on each of 10 of the background squares, taking time to coordinate colours, then appliqué in place, following "Traditional Appliqué Method 1" instructions.

With right sides together, join each heart square to a plain background square, making sure you have 10 blocks with the heart on the left-hand side, and 10 with the heart on the right-hand side. Stitch blocks together to form table runner centre, alternating positions of hearts from block to block (see photograph, this page).

### Border

Measure length of runner top through centre of runner. From border fabric, cut two strips, each 2$^1/_2$" (6.3cm) wide, to this measurement, for side border strips. Join a strip to each side of runner top, easing runner into strip if necessary. Press seam allowances towards runner.

Repeat process to cut and join top and bottom border strips, measuring width of runner after joining side border strips.

### Finishing

With right sides facing, stitch backing pieces together along 20" (51cm) ends. Pin batting to wrong side of runner top, then pin runner top and backing together, right sides facing. Trim sides so that edges are even, and stitch around edges, leaving most of one short side unstitched. Trim seam allowances, turn runner through to right side and slip-stitch opening closed.

Using contrasting quilting thread, sew a cross at each junction of four squares down the centre of the runner. Sew a button over each junction of two squares around the outside of the runner top.

*These perennially cheerful
cushions will do wonders
for a cane chair or sofa ...*

# Flowerpot Cushions

*Inspired by English country appliqué of the past and featuring traditional potplant motifs,*

*these perennially cheerful cushions will do wonders for a cane chair or sofa.*

*In spite of their traditional flavour, the designs can be appliquéd in no time at all using*

*the modern wonder of Vliesofix.*

## MEASUREMENTS

Finished cushion measures approximately 38cm (15") square.

## MATERIALS

- 20cm (8") square each of four different light-coloured cotton prints, for cushion front

- Assorted cotton prints, for appliqué shapes

- 39.5cm (15$\frac{1}{2}$") square of coordinating fabric, for cushion back

- 0.5m x 115cm ($\frac{2}{3}$yd x 45") contrasting fabric, for piping

- 1.5m x 5mm (1$\frac{2}{3}$yds x $\frac{1}{4}$") piping cord

- 0.2m ($\frac{1}{4}$yd) double-sided appliqué webbing, such as Vliesofix

- Coordinating machine thread

- Overdyed/variegated perle cotton No. 8 or stranded embroidery cotton, in contrasting colours

- Small embroidery needle

- 40cm (16") cushion insert

## APPLIQUÉ OUTLINES

Before proceeding, read through "Super Quick Appliqué" on page 114. Appliqué design outlines for both cushions are printed full size on the pattern sheet. Trace outlines for all appliqué shapes in the chosen design — hearts, flowerpot base and top, bird body and wing, stems, flower circles, flower centres and petals (Design 1), and leaves — directly onto Vliesofix. Some parts of the design are made up of several overlapping shapes, each of which needs to be traced separately; trace around the broken lines. Some shapes are used more than once; use the design outline as a guide to check this. Note that design outlines have been printed in reverse so that when shapes are applied to fabric they will be the right way round.

Seam allowances are **not** included on outlines for appliqué shapes, as the shapes are fused into place and the raw edges covered by buttonhole stitch. $^{1}/_{4}$" (6mm) seam allowance is **included** in all other measurements.

## SEWING

### Piecing Cushion Front

With right sides facing, join the 8" (20cm) squares of light-coloured fabric together into two rows of two squares, press seam allowances to one side. Join two rows together, taking care to match

*Flowerpot Cushion Design 1*

*Flowerpot
Cushion
Design 2*

corners exactly, to form 15¹/₂" (39.5cm) square cushion front. Press seam allowances to one side.

### Appliqué

Lightly trace the chosen appliqué design outline onto the cushion front. Centre the design and place the flowerpot 1" (2.5cm) up from the lower edge. Following "Super Quick Appliqué" instructions, fuse appliqué shapes in position. Pay attention to the way in which pieces are layered, referring back to the design outline, where concealed edges are indicated by broken lines.

Using the variegated perle cotton or two strands of embroidery cotton, work blanket stitch (see page 119) around all raw edges of the appliqué shapes.

### Finishing

Using a glass as a template, round off corners on cushion front and back.

Referring to "Bias Binding" on page 118, from piping fabric, cut 1¹/₂" (3.7cm) bias strips, and join to make a total length of 1.5m (1²/₃yds). Following instructions on page 119, make corded piping, trimming seam allowances to ¹/₄" (6mm). Using a zipper foot and beginning at one corner, apply piping to the edges of appliquéd cushion front, overlapping the ends to finish.

With right sides together, stitch cushion front to cushion back around edges, leaving an opening on one edge for turning. Turn cover right side out, press. Place cushion insert inside cover and slip-stitch opening closed.

On happy days
when I can stitch
my life runs smooth
without a hitch

*This cushion would blend
in well with a country
decorating scheme ...*

# Stitcher's Cushion

*This cushion introduces embroidery — a simple back-stitch — into the*

*patchwork and appliqué mix. With its muted greens and pinks*

*and fabric-scrap border, it would blend in well with*

*a country decorating scheme.*

## MEASUREMENTS

Finished cushion measures 49.5cm (19$^1$/$_2$") square.

## MATERIALS

- 31cm (12$^1$/$_4$") square beige and cream cotton check, for centre square
- 0.7m x 115cm ($^3$/$_4$yd x 45") beige and cream floral print, for corner triangles and back
- Small amount each of approximately 24 cotton prints, including six greenish prints, for appliqué shapes
- Tiny amount each of approximately 45 coordinating cotton prints (use as many or as few as you like), for tumbler border
- 52cm (20$^1$/$_2$") square of cream cotton, for front lining
- 52cm (20$^1$/$_2$") square of thin batting

- Coordinating machine thread
- Stranded embroidery cotton in colour that coordinates with appliqué fabrics but contrasts with centre square fabric
- Embroidery needle
- Quilting thread
- Quilting needles (betweens)
- Template plastic or cardboard
- Four x 2cm buttons
- 50cm (20") cushion insert

## APPLIQUÉ AND EMBROIDERY OUTLINES, AND TEMPLATE

Before proceeding, read through "Traditional Appliqué Method 1" on page 114. The appliqué design and embroidery outline are printed full-size on the pattern sheet. Trace onto paper 18 petals and six flower centres. The tumbler template is printed on this page. Referring to "Making Templates" on page 114, trace onto template plastic or cardboard and cut out.

## CUTTING

Remember to **add** $^1/_4$" (6mm) seam allowance to all appliqué shapes before cutting. $^1/_4$" (6mm) seam allowance is **included** on tumbler template and in all other measurements.

From each of six greenish appliqué fabrics, cut a $1^1/_2$" (3.7cm) bias strip, for stems. You will need the following lengths: 2 x $2^1/_2$" (6.3cm), 4" (10cm), $4^3/_4$" (12cm), $8^1/_4$" (20.8cm) and $8^3/_4$" (22cm).

From beige and cream floral print, cut two squares, each $9^1/_2$" (24cm). Cut across each square diagonally to form four corner triangles.

From selection of border fabrics, cut 76 tumbler shapes from tumbler template.

## SEWING

### Piecing Cushion Front

Fold centre square in half to find centre of one side and finger press to mark. Fold a corner triangle in half and finger press to mark centre of long side. With right sides together and centre points matching, join long side of one triangle to one side of centre square. Repeat to join a second triangle to opposing side of square. Open out triangles and press seam allowances away from centre square. Join remaining triangles to other sides of square in same way, making sure seams meet neatly at the ends.

### Embroidery and Appliqué

Lightly trace appliqué design and verse onto centre diamond. Using three strands of embroidery cotton, back-stitch (see page 119) the lettering.

Press under raw edges of each stem strip so that they meet in centre. Refer to "Traditional Appliqué Method 1" when appliquéing shapes onto cushion front. Pin stems in position. Rather than appliqué stitch, work small running stitches in cream quilting thread along both sides of stems to secure. Pin petals in position, then secure using running stitch. Pin flower centres in position, covering raw edges of stems and petals. When appliquéing flower centres, where there are multiple layers of fabric, use back-stitch, leaving gaps between stitches so that result looks like running stitch.

### Tumbler Border

With right sides together, join tumbler blocks to form four border strips: two of approximately 17" (43cm) and two of approximately 20" (51cm). Measure width of cushion through centre and trim ends of shorter border strips to this measurement. With right sides together, join these strips to top and bottom of cushion centre, press seam allowances towards border. Measure length of cushion, trim longer border strips to this measurement, join a strip to each side of cushion front, pressing seam allowances outwards.

### Finishing

Referring to "Layering Quilt" on page 116, baste cushion front, batting and front lining together.

Hand quilt (see page 117) in-the-ditch around the tumber border and along the sides of the diamond that are not covered by appliqué.

From beige floral fabric, cut two backs, each $12^3/_4$" x $20^1/_2$" (32.5cm x 52cm). Press under a double 1" (2.5cm) hem along one long edge of each back, stitch close to fold. Make four evenly spaced buttonholes along one hem, with outer two buttonholes approximately $3^1/_4$" (8.2cm) from sides. Sew buttons onto hem of other back piece to correspond.

Button backs together, then, with right sides up, pin backs together at sides. The back should measure $20^1/_2$" (52cm) square.

With right sides facing, stitch cushion front and back together around edges. Turn cover through to right side, place insert inside cover and button up.

# Quilted
# Cushion

# Quilted Cushion

*In this elegant and understated cushion, a simple*

*potplant quilting design is combined with a subtly coloured patchwork border.*

## MEASUREMENTS

Finished cushion measures approximately 60cm (24") square.

## MATERIALS

- 38cm x 50cm (15" x 20") each of four light-coloured and four dark-coloured printed fabrics, for pieced border blocks

- 0.8m x 115cm (1yd x 45") cream cotton, for quilted centre and front lining

- 0.8m x 115cm (1yd x 45") coordinating printed fabric, for back

- 65cm (25$^1$/$_2$") square of lightweight batting

- 0.3m x 115cm ($^1$/$_3$yd x 45") contrasting fabric, for binding

- Coordinating machine thread

- Quilting thread

- Quilting needles (betweens)

- Four x 2cm buttons

- 60cm (24") cushion insert

## SEWING

### Pieced Border

The border comprises 14 each of alternating nine-patch blocks and shoofly blocks. Each block consists of a light and a dark fabric. Before cutting, arrange border fabrics into light and dark pairs.

**Nine-patch blocks:** From each of border fabrics in three pairs, cut three 1$^1$/$_2$" (3.7cm) strips across width of fabric piece. Reserve one pair of border fabrics and leftover fabric from one pair of cut fabrics for shoofly blocks.

Following directions for quick piecing nine-patch blocks on page 116, stitch strips together in groups of three, then cross-cut into 1$^1$/$_2$" (3.7cm) segments. Stitch segments in two versions of the nine-patch block — see **Diagram 1**. From each set of pieced strips you will be able to make six nine-patch blocks; repeat process to make 14 nine-patch blocks (there will be some segments left over).

1

**Shoofly blocks:** From reserved and uncut pair of border fabrics (four fabrics in total), cut 56 squares (14 from each fabric), each $1^7/_8''$ (4.7cm), for corner half-square triangles. From each of two light fabrics, cut 16 squares, each $1^1/_2''$ (4.7cm), and from each of two dark fabrics, cut 19 squares, each $1^1/_2''$ (4.7cm), for remaining squares in block. For each shoofly block, you will need either one central square of dark fabric and four of light fabric, or one central square of light fabric and four of dark fabric.

Following instructions for making half-square triangle units on page 115, make 56 units for corners, using light and dark squares for each unit.

Referring to **Diagram 2**, join squares and half-square triangle units together in rows, then join rows to complete shoofly block. Make 14 shoofly blocks.

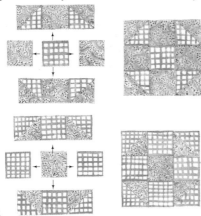

2

### Assembling Cushion Front

From cream cotton, cut an $18^1/_2''$ (47cm) square, for quilted centre.

Alternating nine-patch blocks and shoofly blocks, lay out blocks in two rows of six and two rows of eight, in a border formation (**Diagram 3**). With right sides facing, join blocks together. Join the six-block border strips to quilted centre, then join the eight-block strips. Press seam allowances towards border.

The assembled cushion front should measure $24^1/_2''$ (62.3cm) square, including seam allowances.

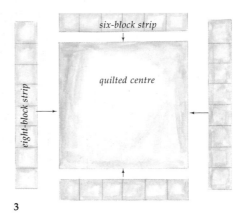

six-block strip

quilted centre

eight-block strip

3

### Quilting

The quilting pattern is printed on the pattern sheet. Referring to "Marking Quilting Patterns" on page 116, transfer quilting pattern to cushion centre.

From cream cotton, cut a $24^1/_2''$ (62.3cm) square, for front lining. Referring to "Layering Quilt" on page 116, baste cushion front, batting and lining together.

Following directions in "Hand Quilting" on page 117, quilt central motif. Quilt in-the-ditch along outer edge of quilted centre, then make another row of quilting 1" (2.5cm) inside this line.

### Finishing

From floral fabric, cut two rectangles, each $14^3/_4'' \times 24^1/_2''$ (37.5cm x 62.3cm), for backs.

Press under a double 1" (2.5cm) hem along one long edge of each back, stitch close to fold. Make four evenly spaced buttonholes along one hem, with the outer two buttonholes approximately 4" (10cm) from the sides. Sew buttons onto hem of other back piece to correspond.

Button backs together, then, with right sides up, pin backs together at sides. Back should measure $24^1/_2''$ (62.3cm) square.

With wrong sides facing, pin then stitch cushion front and back together around edges, allowing $1/_8''$ (3mm) seam.

Following directions for "Straight Binding: Double" on page 118, cut strips from binding fabric, join and apply to cushion edges.

Place insert inside cover and button up.

*Pastel prints with a 1930s feel add charm and whimsy to a functional item ...*

# Heart Sewing Box

*Pastel prints with a 1930s feel add charm and whimsy to a functional item. But you don't have to make a special purchase; leftover fabric scraps cleverly combined would look just as good.*

## MEASUREMENTS

Finished box measures 22cm x 16cm x 10cm high ($8^3/_4$" x $6^3/_8$" x 4").

## MATERIALS

- 10cm x 20cm (4" x 8") each of five different cotton prints, for appliqué hearts
- 20cm x 25cm (8" x 10") each of 20 cotton prints, for lid, back and front, nine-patch sides, base and all linings
- Small amount fibrefill
- 50cm x 75cm (20" x 30") cotton batting

- Coordinating machine thread
- Stranded embroidery cotton in five bright colours
- Needles: embroidery and tapestry
- Ten two-hole buttons in different colours
- Template plastic or stiff cardboard
- Glue-stick

### TEMPLATES

Templates for appliqué hearts and base/lid are printed on the pattern sheet. Make a cardboard or plastic template of the heart, and two of the base/lid — one of the cutting line and one of the sewing line.

### SEWING

**Note:** *$^1/_4$" (6mm) seam allowance is **included** on heart template, and in all measurements.*

### *Appliqué*

From each of the five appliqué fabrics, cut two hearts.

We used a version of the "No-turn Appliqué" method (see page 114) to apply the hearts to the box. With right sides facing, stitch same-fabric heart shapes together around edges, leaving small opening for turning. Clip seam allowances, turn each heart through to right side, and stuff with small amount of fibrefill. Slip-stitch opening closed.

### Lid

From each of two cotton prints, cut one base/lid with seam allowance, for lid and lid lining.

From batting, cut one base/lid with seam allowance.

From cardboard or template plastic, cut one base/lid without seam allowance, for lid insert.

Pin three hearts to right side of lid piece, using outlines on base/lid template as guide. Using three strands of embroidery cotton and a different colour for each heart, blanket stitch (see page 119) hearts in place. Set two remaining hearts aside.

Pin batting piece to wrong side of lid piece. With right sides facing and raw edges even, pin lid/batting to lid lining. Stitch along four edges, leaving back edge and adjacent side edge open. Trim corners and batting, turn lid through to right side. Place insert inside lid. Pin side edge closed, turning top seam allowance over and bottom seam allowance under insert. Leave back edge open.

Using three strands of embroidery cotton, work blanket stitch around stitched *and* pinned edges of lid. Insert needle $1/4''$ (6mm) from the edge on top, angling the needle so that it emerges just below seam line; avoid sewing through the insert.

### Back and Front

From each of four cotton prints, cut a rectangle, $4^1/4''$ x $4^1/2''$ (10.7cm x 11.4cm), for back and front, and back and front linings.

From batting, cut two rectangles, each $4^1/4''$ x $4^1/2''$ (10.7cm x 11.4cm).

From cardboard or template plastic, cut two rectangles, each $3^3/4''$ x $4''$ (9.5cm x 10cm), for back and front inserts.

Pin a heart onto centre of right side of back piece and front piece, and blanket stitch in place.

Baste batting rectangle to wrong side of back piece. With right sides facing, stitch back/batting and lid together along upper edge of back (**Diagram 1a**), catching in seam allowance of lid and lid lining but avoiding lid insert. Open out back. Pin back lining to back/batting, right sides facing and raw edges even, and stitch down side edges, starting and finishing $1/4''$ (6mm) from raw edges (**Diagram 1b**).

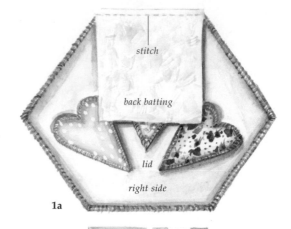

**1a**

**1b**

Turn back through to the right side, fold down upper seam allowance to cover raw edges and slip-stitch upper opening closed. Leave lower edge open.

Baste remaining batting rectangle to wrong side of front piece. Pin front/batting to front lining, right sides facing and raw edges even, then stitch together along two short edges and one long edge, starting and finishing exactly $1/4''$ (6mm) from raw edges. Trim corners, turn through to right side and press.

### Nine-patch Sides

From each of four cotton prints, cut five $1^3/4''$ (4.5cm) squares, and from each of four different cotton prints, cut four $1^3/4''$ (4.5cm) squares, for nine-patch sides.

From each of four different cotton prints, cut a $4^1/4''$ (10.7cm) square, for side linings.

From batting, cut four squares, each $4^1/_4''$ (10.7cm).

From cardboard or template plastic, cut four squares, each $3^3/_4''$ (9.5cm), for side inserts.

For each nine-patch block you will need four $1^3/_4''$ (4.5cm) squares of one fabric and five $1^3/_4''$ (4.5cm) squares of a different fabric. With right sides facing, join squares together in three rows of three, alternating fabrics, to make a nine-patch block (see photograph on page 102). Press seams towards darker fabrics. Repeat, using remaining squares, to make four nine-patch blocks in total.

Baste batting square to wrong side of each nine-patch block, then pin each nine-patch block/batting and side lining together, right sides facing and raw edges even. Stitch around three edges, starting and stopping $^1/_4''$ (6mm) from raw edge. Trim corners, turn through to right side and press.

### Joining Front, Back and Sides to Base

From a cotton print, cut one base/lid with seam allowance, for base.

On right side of base piece, mark each corner point of seam allowance with a dot. With right sides together, pin a nine-patch side to one edge of base, catching in right-side seam allowance *only* (**Diagram 2**). Stitch in place, starting and finishing exactly $^1/_4''$ (6mm) from corners; avoid catching the lining seam allowance in the seam.

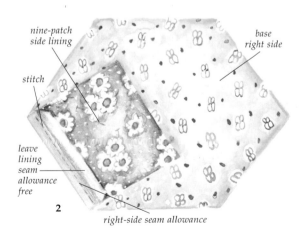

nine-patch side lining

stitch

leave lining seam allowance free

2

base right side

right-side seam allowance

Stitch another nine-patch side to adjacent edge of base in same way, keeping stitching between dots and ensuring seams meet. Repeat to join

remaining nine-patch sides to other side edges of base, and the front and back (with lid attached) to front and back edges of base.

Using three strands of embroidery cotton in chosen colour, blanket stitch a nine-patch side to box back. Begin at the base, sew up the side edges and continue along upper edge of nine-patch side. Using three strands of cotton in another colour, blanket stitch first nine-patch side to adjacent nine-patch side, again continuing blanket stitch along upper edge of second nine-patch side. Continue around box base in this way, changing colour of embroidery cotton for each side, until box "wall" is complete.

Place appropriate inserts in side, front and back pockets, trimming to fit if necessary. Working from inside of box, baste the lower open edges of the front, back and sides together, to secure inserts.

### Base Lining

From a cotton print, cut one base/lid with seam allowance, for base lining.

From batting, cut two bases/lids without seam allowance.

From cardboard or template plastic, cut a base/lid without seam allowance, for base lining insert.

Turn box inside out, being careful not to bend the cardboard. Trim $^1/_8''$ (3mm) off all edges of base insert using a rotary cutter. Trim the two pieces of batting to the same size. Using a glue-stick, attach one piece of batting to the insert. Position base lining on batting, wrong side against batting, and turn seam allowances of base lining over the insert; glue in place. Glue remaining piece of batting to the insert side of the base, covering the raw edges of the fabric. Push completed base lining into bottom of box, gluing to secure if you wish.

### Finishing

Thread a needle with 60cm length of embroidery cotton, pulling ends equal. Take needle down through centre front of lid, reinsert in same hole, creating a loop. Pass all threads through loop, pull gently to tighten. Cut needle from thread. Thread buttons onto thread lengths, knot ends together.

*These pincushions would make excellent gifts for quilter friends ...*

# Pincushions

*These pincushions would make excellent gifts for quilter friends.*

## Log Cabin Pincushion

### MEASUREMENTS

Finished pincushion measures 13.3cm (5$^1$/$_4$") square.

### MATERIALS

- Small amount each of 17 different cotton prints, for log cabin block
- 15cm (6") square of plain fabric, for backing
- Polyester fibrefill
- Coordinating machine thread
- Stranded embroidery cotton in colour that contrasts with backing
- Embroidery needle
- Large, decorative button

### CUTTING

**Note:** $^1$/$_4$" *(6mm) seam allowance is* **included** *in all measurements.*

From one cotton print, cut one 1$^1$/$_4$" (3cm) square, for pincushion centre.

From each of remaining cotton prints, cut a strip, 1" x 6" (2.5cm x 15cm), for log cabin block.

### SEWING

With right sides together and raw edges even, stitch a strip of fabric to one side of centre square (see **Diagram** on following page). Trim the strip so that it is exactly the same length as the square. Press seam allowances away from the square.

Join a second strip across cut end of first strip and along second side of square. Trim end so that it is even with edge of square, press seam allowances away from square.

Proceed around the square, joining third and fourth strips, and pressing all seam allowances away from centre. This completes one round of log cabin.

Continue in this manner, joining strips in order indicated on **Diagram** until block is complete.

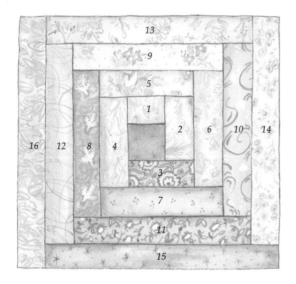

Measure the completed log cabin block and trim the backing fabric to the same size.

With right sides together, stitch log cabin block and backing together around edges, leaving a 2" (5cm) opening on one side. Turn through to the right side, and stuff firmly with fibrefill. Slip-stitch opening closed.

Position button in centre of log cabin block. Bring three strands of embroidery cotton through from back of pincushion, leaving a 2" (5cm) tail, and fasten button as you take thread through to the back again. Tie a firm knot at the back while pulling gently to embed button in the cushion, trim ends to approximately 1" (2.5cm).

# Personalised Pincushion

## MEASUREMENTS

Finished pincushion measures approximately 16.5cm x 19cm ($6^1/_2$" x $7^1/_2$").

## MATERIALS

- Tiny amount each of 26 different cotton prints, for patched border

- 12.5cm x 15cm (5" x 6") closely woven linen or raw silk in pale colour, for pincushion centre

- 17.5cm x 20cm (7" x 8") ticking, for back

- Coordinating machine thread

- Stranded embroidery cotton in contrasting colour

- Embroidery needle

## CUTTING

**Note:** $^1/_4$" (6mm) seam allowance is **included** in all measurements.

From each cotton print, cut a $1^1/_2$" (3.7cm) square.

## SEWING

Using light pencil, write chosen name onto centre of linen. Using one strand of embroidery cotton, work stem stitch (see page 119) over outline.

With right sides together, join printed cotton squares to form four strips, three of seven squares and one of five squares.

With right sides together and raw edges even, join the five-square strip to one short side of pincushion centre. Trim ends so that they are even with edges of pincushion centre, press seam allowances away from centre. Join a seven-square strip to each of the long sides, trim ends, press seams towards strips. Then join the last strip to the remaining side.

With right sides facing, stitch pincushion front and back together around edges, leaving 2" (5cm) opening on one side. Turn through to right side, stuff with fibrefill. Slip-stitch opening closed.

# Quilter's
# Carry Bag

# Quilter's Carry Bag

*Every patchworker and quilter needs something in which to carry fabrics and equipment,*

*and this bag fits the bill — it's amply proportioned and provides all the necessary*

*pockets. There is no need to replicate the patchwork design shown; it's more fun to create*

*your own. Alternatively, if you have any patchwork offcuts (or orphan blocks)*

*that you would like to display, this bag is the perfect canvas. Then again, you could use*

*plain fabric throughout as a backdrop to your own quilting designs.*

## MEASUREMENTS

Finished bag measures approximately 49.5cm x 65cm (19$^1$/$_2$" x 25$^1$/$_2$").

## MATERIALS

- Assorted fabrics, 1.5m x 115cm (1$^2$/$_3$yds x 45") in total, for bag front and back patchwork

- Three different printed fabrics, 1m x 115cm (1$^1$/$_4$yds x 45") in total, for pocket linings and inner pocket

- 0.7m x 115cm ($^3$/$_4$yd x 45") dark printed fabric, for bag lining

- 0.6m x 115cm ($^3$/$_4$yd x 45") fabric, for straps

- 1.3m (1$^1$/$_2$yd) square of thin cotton batting

- Coordinating machine thread

- Contrasting machine thread

- Quilting thread and needles (optional)

- Three large wooden buttons

## SEWING

We have provided measurements for all sections of the bag — the back, top front pocket Side A, top front pocket Side B, and lower front pocket. We suggest you make a patchwork piece, in any style, or cut a readymade patchwork piece to size, for each section.

### Back

**Note:** $^1/_4$" (6mm) seam allowance is **included** in all measurements.

All back pieces should be made or cut to measure 20" x 26" (51cm x 66cm).

Using selected fabrics, make a rectangle of patchwork to back measurements.

From batting, cut a rectangle to back measurements.

Centre batting on wrong side of patchwork back, baste layers together. Referring to "Quilting" on page 117, quilt as desired by hand or machine.

### Top Front (Vertical) Pocket

All pieces for Side A should be made or cut to measure $11^1/_2$" x $16^1/_4$" (29cm x 41.2cm), while pieces for Side B should be made or cut to measure 10" x $16^1/_4$" (25cm x 41.2cm).

Using selected fabrics, make a rectangle of patchwork to Side A measurements and another to Side B measurements.

From batting, cut a rectangle to each of Side A and Side B measurements.

From a pocket lining fabric, cut a rectangle to each of Side A and Side B measurements.

From contrasting fabric, cut a strip, $2^1/_2$" x $16^1/_4$" (6.3cm x 41.2cm), for binding edge of Side B.

Centre batting on wrong side of Side A lining, then place Side A patchwork on top, right side up. Pin then baste layers together. Repeat process to baste Side B patchwork, batting and lining together. Quilt Side A and Side B as desired.

Trim batting back $^1/_4$" (6mm) along right-hand (long) edge of Side A. Fold edge of lining over to enclose batting. Turn under raw edge of patchwork top, pin to lining. Slip-stitch folded edges of top and lining together (see "Folded Finish" on page 118).

Fold binding strip in half lengthwise, wrong sides together. With right sides together and raw edges even, stitch binding to left-hand edge of Side B. Press binding over raw edge of batting and slip-stitch folded edge to lining, $^1/_4$" (6mm) in from raw edge.

Work a buttonhole halfway down centre front on Side B.

With right sides up, overlap B over A by about 2" (5cm); centre of binding should align with centre front, and total width, including seam allowances, should be 20" (51cm) (**Diagram 1**). Baste to hold.

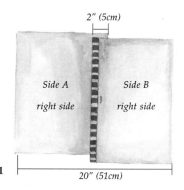

### Lower Front Pocket

All pieces for lower front pocket should be made or cut to measure 20" x $10^1/_4$" (51cm x 26cm).

Using selected fabrics, make a rectangle of patchwork to lower pocket measurements.

From batting, cut a rectangle to lower pocket measurements.

From each of two pocket lining fabrics, cut a rectangle to lower pocket measurements.

From a dark fabric, cut a strip, $2^1/_2$" x 20" (6.3cm x 51cm), for binding top edge of pocket.

Centre batting on wrong side of one pocket lining, then place patchwork piece on top, right side up. Pin then baste layers together. Quilt as desired.

Fold binding strip in half lengthwise, wrong sides facing. With right sides together and raw edges even, stitch binding strip to top (long) edge of pocket. Press binding over batting and slip-stitch folded edge to lining, $^1/_4$" (6mm) in from raw edge.

Work two buttonholes in the top edge, $4^3/_4$" (12cm) from each side of the pocket.

With right sides facing, stitch remaining pocket lining to lower edge of top front pocket. Press open lining, position completed lower pocket on front of bag (**Diagram 2**), and secure to lining by stitching around sides and bottom.

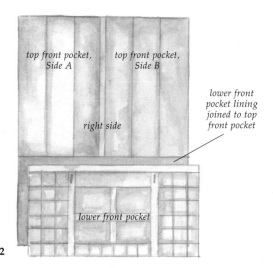

2

## Joining Front and Back

With right sides together and raw edges even, stitch bag front to back around side and bottom edges. Turn through to right side.

## Lining and Inner Pocket for Rulers

From bag lining fabric, cut two rectangles, each 20" x 26" (51cm x 66cm).

From inner pocket fabric, cut a rectangle, 8" x 24" (20.2cm x 61cm).

Press under $^1/_4$" (6mm), then 1" (2.5cm) along one short side of inner pocket, stitch hem in place. Press under $^1/_2$" (1.2cm) along other short side, stitch, then press under $^1/_4$" (6mm) along each long side. With right sides up, position pocket on left-hand side of one lining piece, top-stitch in place down both long sides (**Diagram 3**).

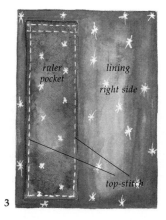

3

With right sides together, stitch front to back lining around sides and bottom edge. Without turning, place lining inside bag, with ruler pocket at back, and baste lining to bag around upper edges.

## Binding

From one of assorted fabrics, cut a strip, $2^1/_2$" x $42^1/_2$" (6.3cm x 108cm), for binding upper edge of bag.

Press binding strip in half lengthwise, wrong sides together. Apply binding to upper edge of bag, referring to Diagrams 13b and 13d and instructions on page 118 for "Straight Binding: Double" when beginning and ending stitching. Turn binding over edge of bag and slip-stitch folded edge to lining.

## Straps and Finishing

From strap fabric, cut two strips, each 5" x 42" (13cm x 107cm).

Fold each strap in half lengthwise, right sides together, and stitch down long side. Turn through to right side. Using contrasting thread, stitch rows $^1/_4$" (6mm) apart along length of strap.

Position ends of one strap on outside front of bag and ends of other strap on outside back, with each strap end $1^3/_4$" (4.5cm) from upper edge and $3^3/_4$" (9.5cm) from a side seam, and raw edges pointing towards top of bag (**Diagram 4**). Stitch ends in place.

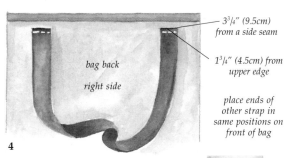

4

Fold straps over so that they cover raw edges, and stitch a square to hold each end in place (**Diagram 5**).

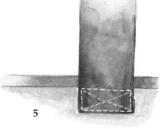

5

Sew on wooden buttons to correspond with buttonhole in top front pocket and buttonholes in lower front pocket.

# General Instructions

## MATERIALS AND TOOLS

### Fabrics

The most suitable patchwork and quilting fabric is lightweight pure cotton, especially for the beginner quiltmaker. Silks, satins and velvets can be used for special effects, but they should be used with care. Some fabrics should be avoided altogether. For example, polycotton and heavy fabrics such as canvas tend to be too closely woven for ease of quilting, while open-weave fabrics are too transparent and tend to fray. Stretch fabrics are difficult to control and will pucker.

Select fully washable fabrics for items that will be subject to regular washing, and try not to combine fabrics that need to be dry-cleaned with those that need to be washed. In general, you will achieve the best result if you combine fabrics with the same fibre content. Check also that the backing fabric is similar in weight and fibre content to the fabrics used in the quilt top. For a hand-quilted backing, soft cotton is ideal, as it is easy to stitch through.

Wash fabrics separately in warm water with mild soap or fabric softener before cutting them to avoid shrinking the finished item in later washings and to test for colour fastness. If dye leaks out, continue to rinse until water runs clear. Discard fabrics that continue to bleed after several rinses. When fabric is dry, pull gently to straighten grain, then press.

### Batting

All quilts need some form of batting, or wadding, to form the centre of the quilt sandwich (top, batting and backing). Batting is available in cotton, wool and polyester. When choosing batting, take into account washability and loft, or thickness, and the recommended spacing between quilting lines. Choose a batting that has been bonded, which is a process that prevents loose fibres working their way through the fabric and producing an unsightly effect known as "bearding".

**Polyester batting** The most commonly available batting, this comes in a range of thicknesses, washes well and is very economical.

**Pure cotton batting** This is low-loft, giving a flatter appearance to the quilt, and is therefore preferred by quiltmakers aiming to create the look of an antique. Until recently cotton batting required close quilting to prevent it from becoming lumpy when washed, but now there is a cotton batting available that has been needle punched, which is a process that prevents lumpiness. When buying cotton batting, check whether it is suitable for hand or machine quilting. To prevent shrinkage, wash quilts with cotton batting in cold water.

**Cotton/polyester batting** This offers the low loft and density of cotton batting while costing less. It should be washed in cold water.

**Wool batting** This results in a warm quilt that drapes well, and it is generally easy to quilt; however, wool fibres sometimes migrate through the patchwork or quilting lines.

### Cutting Tools

**Scissors** Use paper scissors for cutting paper, cardboard and template plastic, and a sharp pair of fabric scissors for cutting fabrics. For clipping appliqué, use a pair of small scissors with sharp points.

**Rotary cutter** A single-blade large rotary cutter is recommended for fast and accurate cutting of strips and squares. You will also need a self-healing rotary cutting mat, a set square and a quilter's ruler.

### Marking Tools

There are many markers that can be used to mark the quilting pattern on the fabric, including 2B propelling pencils designed especially for this purpose. Experiment with well-sharpened soft lead pencils, chinagraph pencils, water-soluble crayons, blunt needles (for pale or shiny fabrics), hardened soap slivers or silverpoint pencils. You need a marker that provides a clear, crisp line and can be washed out or removed on completion of quilting. Always test marker on fabric first.

### Quilting and Sewing Supplies

**Pins** Sharp, glass-headed pins are the best to use for piecing, while 4cm ($1^1/2''$) safety pins are the most suitable for pin-basting.

**Needles** Use crewel, or embroidery, needles for hand piecing and appliqué, and a long thin needle for basting. For hand quilting, you will need a range of betweens, which are very short, stubby needles. If you are new to quilting, you might feel most comfortable with an 8 or a 9, which is at the longer end of the range.

**Thread** Use cotton thread for hand piecing and appliqué; polycotton thread is stronger than the fabric and eventually cuts through the quilt. There is a special quilting thread available for hand and machine quilting. Alternatively, for hand quilting, you could wax an ordinary cotton thread to prevent it from knotting; beeswax cakes are available for this purpose.

**Thimbles** Some quilters prefer to work without a thimble on the hand underneath the quilt so that they can feel and guide the needle when it pierces the quilt backing. A compromise would be to tape the middle finger of this hand with masking tape, which protects it while allowing it to deflect the needle. A leather thimble is another alternative. Generally, a metal quilter's thimble with a ridge is used on the middle finger of the top hand.

**Hoop** For hand quilting, a free-standing quilting hoop is needed to keep the area being worked taut. Choose a round hoop rather than an oval one, as it gives a more even tension.

## APPLIQUÉ METHODS

Use whichever method you prefer, although we have indicated which we think more suitable to use in particular projects.

### Traditional Appliqué Method 1

Lightly trace appliqué design onto background fabric with a pencil. Trace each appliqué shape onto paper and cut out. Pin each paper shape, face down, onto wrong side of appropriate fabric, then cut shapes from fabric, adding $1/4$" (6mm) seam allowance. Clip curves and Vs.

Turn seam allowance over edge of paper and baste in place through both layers. (For circular shapes, run a gathering stitch around the outside in seam line, then pull up gathers to turn seam allowance over template.) Pin or baste shapes to background fabric. Sew in place with small hemming stitches in matching thread, catching only the folded edge of each shape. Sew to within $3/4$" (2cm) of starting point, remove basting, remove paper with tweezers and finish stitching.

### Traditional Appliqué Method 2

Trace appliqué design onto background fabric with a pencil. Trace each appliqué piece onto firm paper and cut out. Draw around each shape on right side of fabric and remove pattern piece. Cut shapes from fabric, adding $1/4$" (6mm) seam allowance.

Turn the seam allowance under, following the pencil line and basting in place as you go. Pin each basted shape to background fabric and sew in place with small hemming stitches, catching only the folded edge of the shape.

### No-turn Appliqué

Cut all appliqué shapes, with a $1/4$" (6mm) seam allowance, from both chosen fabric and a backing fabric, taking care to cut mirror pairs. With right sides facing, stitch shapes together around edges, leaving a small opening for turning. Clip curves, turn right side out, slip-stitch opening closed, and press. Sew these shapes to background, using desired embroidery stitch.

### Super Quick Appliqué

Trace appliqué outlines onto the smooth paper side of double-sided fusible webbing (such as Vliesofix), leaving about $1/2$" (1.2cm) between each shape. Cut out roughly and place each traced shape, pencil side up, on wrong side of chosen appliqué fabrics. Press with a hot iron, making sure edges are securely fused. (This will result in a reversed image. If you want image the right way round, flip outline before tracing.) Cut out each shape accurately along traced lines.

Remove backing paper and place shapes in position, right side up, on background fabric. Fuse shapes in place with a hot iron. Edges can be left unstitched, but to make them more durable and attractive, finish with machine appliqué (a close, narrow zigzag), or blanket stitch or another embroidery stitch, by hand.

## PATCHWORK TECHNIQUES

### Making Templates

Trace pattern onto template plastic, marking corners with dots and joining using ruler and pen. Cut out using a craft knife and steel ruler. To make a template that grips the fabric, trace shape onto paper, medium-grade sandpaper and plastic. Glue these layers together, with the sandpaper on the bottom and facing outwards and the plastic on top.

### Rotary Cutting

Fold fabric in half lengthwise (with selvedges matching), then fold in half lengthwise again (with folded edge and selvedges matching), press. Place folded fabric on cutting mat, with double fold nearest you and fabric extending to your right (reverse if you are left-handed). Align one of the ruler's horizontal grid lines with the folded edge of the fabric, and place the cutting edge of the ruler slightly in from the raw edges. Pressing down firmly on the ruler with one hand, run the cutter blade through the fabric along the edge of the ruler to trim and straighten the fabric (**Diagram 1**).

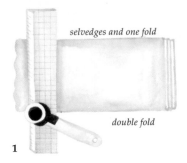

*selvedges and one fold*

*double fold*

**1**

To cut fabric into strips, decide on width of each strip, add seam allowance to both sides, then find the final measurement on the ruler. Place the ruler with this measurement line on the straight cut edge of the fabric and a horizontal line on the fold of the fabric (to prevent you from cutting strips with "V" shapes at the fold). Run the cutter blade along the edge of the ruler (**Diagram 2**). Continue in this manner until you have the required number of strips.

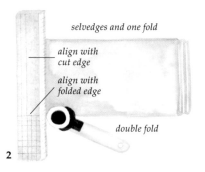

*selvedges and one fold*

*align with cut edge*

*align with folded edge*

*double fold*

**2**

To cut squares, cut a strip to desired width of finished square, plus seam allowances. Place strip across cutting board, place measurement line along one end of strip and horizontal line on lower edge of strip and cut the square (**Diagram 3**).

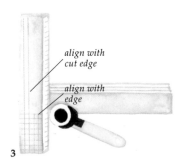

*align with cut edge*

*align with edge*

**3**

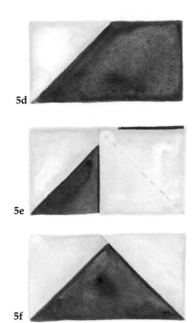

5d

5e

5f

*Piecing Fabrics*

**Hand piecing** With right sides facing and matching marked sewing lines, pin pieces together as shown in **Diagram 4a**. Work small running stitches along pinned sewing line, beginning and ending with a few back-stitches at corners.

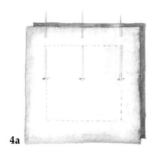

4a

To join rows, place two rows together, right sides facing and seam lines matching. Insert a pin exactly through corners and marked sewing lines (**Diagram 4b**).

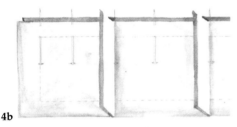

4b

Sew together with running stitch, knotting thread or back-stitching at each seam, then passing needle through seam allowance to other side.

**Machine piecing** Set stitch length at 12–15 stitches per inch. Patchwork or piecing feet are available that indicate a perfect $1/4$" (6mm) seam, for perfect piecing! Alternatively, place masking tape on your machine so that its edge is exactly $1/4$" from the needle and use this as a guide.

With right sides facing, place pieces together and feed under presser foot. Pin only if necessary. There is no need to back-stitch at the end of seams, as most seams will be crossed and held by others.

Use "chain piecing" when stitching multiples of the one unit. Line up several units to be stitched. Stitch first unit as usual, then, rather than back-stitching or cutting thread, feed

in second unit and stitch. Continue in this manner, forming a chain. Clip threads when pressing.

**Pressing** In general, press seam allowances towards the darker fabric to prevent show-through. Keep in mind that the fewer the layers of fabric, the easier it is to quilt, so try to press seams accordingly.

*Some Quick-piecing Methods*

Quick-piecing methods increase accuracy, as well as saving time.

**Flying geese units** For each flying geese unit, you will need a rectangle and two squares. Draw a diagonal line from corner to corner on the wrong side of each square (**Diagram 5a**). With right sides together, position a square on left-hand side of rectangle and stitch on the line (**Diagram 5b**). Trim $1/4$" (6mm) away from the stitching line (**Diagram 5c**) and press triangle open (**Diagram 5d**). With right sides together, place remaining square on the right-hand side of the rectangle, and stitch on the line (**Diagram 5e**). When complete, the point at which the two corner triangles cross is in the centre and $1/4$" (6mm) in from the raw edge to allow for the seam (**Diagram 5f**).

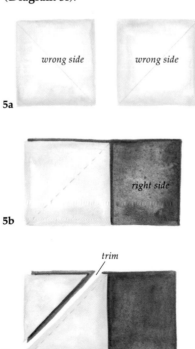

*wrong side*    *wrong side*

5a

*right side*

5b

trim

5c

**Half-square triangle units** For each unit, you will need two squares in contrasting fabrics. With right sides facing and raw edges matching, place squares together with lighter square on top. Draw a diagonal line from corner to corner on uppermost square (**Diagram 6a**). Stitch exactly $1/4$" (6mm) on either side of the pencil line, then cut on the line (**Diagram 6b**). Open out, and press seam towards the darker fabric. You now have two half-square triangle units (**Diagram 6c**).

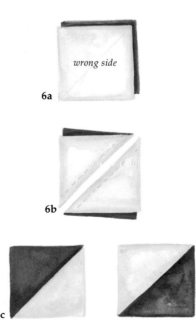

*wrong side*

6a

6b

6c

**Quarter-square triangle units** Pencil a diagonal line that crosses over the seam on wrong side of half-square triangle. Place two half-square triangles together, right sides facing and seams aligning, but with same-fabric triangles in opposing positions (**Diagram 7a**). Stitch exactly $^1/_4$″ (6mm) either side of pencil line, cut along pencil line (**Diagram 7b**) and press seam allowances open. You now have two quarter-square triangle units (**Diagram 7c**).

*wrong side*

**7a**

**7b**

**7c**

**Nine-patch block** Cut three dark and three light strips across width of fabric. Stitch together in two sets of three, reversing order of strips in second set: one set will consist of a light strip stitched in the centre of two dark strips, and one will have a dark strip in between two light strips (**Diagram 8a**). Press seams towards darker fabric — towards centre strip on one set and away from centre strip on other set. Cut sets of three into strips across seams, using same measurement as width of each strip (**Diagram 8b**). Arrange three sets of three patches into a nine-patch block (**Diagram 8c**). The seams will match as they lock together.

**8a**

*cutting lines*

**8b**

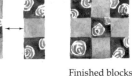

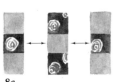

Finished blocks

**8c**

### Foundation Piecing
This method of piecing allows you to achieve accurate blocks, even when working with tiny scraps of fabric. Stitch fabric patches onto a foundation pattern of tracing paper or transparent interfacing, following the seam lines marked on the pattern exactly. When piecing is complete, the foundation paper or fabric can be torn away or left.

### Borders
Before attaching a border, measure the length of the quilt *through the centre* of the quilt top. Cut side border strips to this measurement, and join to quilt top. Then measure width of quilt through centre of quilt top and cut top and bottom border strips to this measurement. Join to top and bottom of quilt top.

## MARKING QUILTING PATTERNS
Mark the quilting pattern on the quilt top before layering the quilt.

### Using Templates or Stencils
Use one of the various markers available (see "Marking Tools", on page 113) to trace around a template or stencil. You can either make your own stencil — by tracing the design onto template plastic and cutting around the outer edge and inner sections of the design — or purchase one of the many commercial stencil designs available.

### Tracing
Draw the design on white paper with a black marker. Position the design over a light source (on a sheet of glass with a table lamp underneath), with fabric on top, tape both layers securely. Trace lines onto fabric with preferred marker.

### Basting
Trace the design onto tissue paper, then lay the pattern paper on the fabric and baste along the lines of the design. Tear the tissue paper away as quilting progresses.

### Using Net
Baste stiff net over the design and draw over lines with a soft pencil. Then pin the net onto the quilt and trace over the pencil lines, using silver pencil, chalk or soapstone.

## LAYERING QUILT
After marking quilting pattern, make a sandwich of the quilt top, batting and backing. If it is necessary to join batting, butt pieces together

(do not overlap them) and whipstitch or work cross-stitches across the join. You can join the backing fabric either across its width or down its length — instructions are provided in individual projects.

Press quilt top and backing. Spread the backing out on a flat surface, wrong side up. Keep it as smooth as possible and, if you can, stretch it slightly, either by pinning it to carpet or by taping it to a hard surface. Centre the batting on top, then position the quilt on top of the two layers. Batting and backing should be approximately 1–1$^1$/$_2$" (2.5–4cm) larger than quilt top all around. Starting from the centre, baste or safety pin layers together. If stitching, work large running stitches (**Diagram 9a**), smoothing layers while working towards the edges. If pinning, use 1$^1$/$_2$" (4cm) safety pins 4–6" (10–15cm) apart (**Diagram 9b**).

**9a**

**9b**

## QUILTING

Apart from its decorative qualities, quilting secures the quilt layers and prevents the batting from shifting.

### Hand Quilting

Place the area to be quilted in the hoop and stretch to an even tension.

Thread the needle with one strand of quilting thread and knot the end. Start quilting in the centre of the quilt and work out towards the sides. Pop the knot through the top and into the batting by giving it a quick tug. Sew through all three layers with a running stitch. The stitch is made with a rocking motion: with a thimble on your middle finger, push the needle down through the quilt until it touches the finger or thimble of the hand underneath. This finger then forces the needle up so that the smallest possible stitch is taken. One stitch at a time can be taken or several stitches can be loaded onto the needle before it is pulled through (**Diagram 10**).

**10**

Concentrate on working small, evenly spaced stitches (unless the project specifies otherwise).

### Machine Quilting

It is preferable to use a walking foot on the machine, otherwise the backing tends to feed through the machine faster than the quilt top. Try to work in long continuous lines; start with in-the-ditch and outline quilting and all-over grids.

## FINISHING

### Self-binding — Back to Front

Cut quilt backing at least 1" (2.5cm) wider all around than quilt top. When layering quilt, trim quilt top and batting evenly. With right side of quilt top uppermost, mark a border around quilt top and batting on wrong side of backing

and trim excess (**Diagram 11a**). The border should be the width of the finished binding plus about $^1$/$_4$" (6mm). Fold quilt corners back so that corner point of backing touches corner point of quilt top and batting. Cut off corner along fold line (**Diagram 11b**). Fold trimmed corner onto quilt top diagonally (**Diagram 11c**). Press under raw edges of backing, then fold backing onto quilt top along one side, pin. Fold adjacent edge onto quilt top, forming a mitre at corner (**Diagram 11d**). Slip-stitch folded edges of binding to quilt top, and mitred edges together at corners. Continue with other sides.

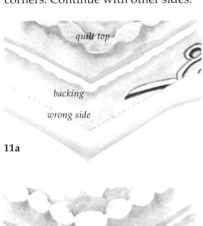

**11a**

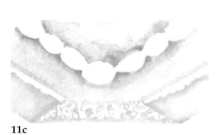

**11b**

**11c**

**11d**

### Folded Finish

Trim quilt top, backing and batting so that they are even, then trim batting back $^1/_4''$ (6mm). Fold edges of backing over to enclose batting (**Diagram 12**). Turn under raw edges of quilt top and pin to backing. Slip-stitch folded edges of top and backing together.

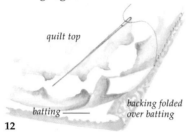

quilt top

batting

backing folded over batting

**12**

### Straight Binding

Note that you should always use a straight binding (as opposed to bias binding) on straight-edged quilts to avoid any stretching of quilt edges. It is also preferable to use double binding on quilt edges, as it is more durable than single binding and easier to attach.

**Double** Measure the depth of binding that will show on the quilt top      , multiply this figure by 4 and add on $^1/_2''$ (1.2cm) for seam allowance. This gives you the cutting width of the binding.

Fold binding fabric in half from selvedge to selvedge, and, using quilter's ruler and rotary cutter, square off fabric at 90° to selvedges. Cut enough binding strips across width of fabric to go around outer edge of quilt, plus extra for mitres, seam allowances and ease.

With right sides facing, stitch strips together on the diagonal along short edges (**Diagram 13a**), to make one continuous strip of binding. Trim seam allowance to $^1/_4''$ (6mm) and press seams open.

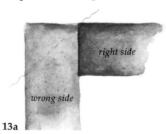

right side

wrong side

**13a**

With wrong sides together, fold and press binding in half lengthwise. At one end of binding, open strip out and fold end down on the diagonal, press (**Diagram 13b**). Trim edge $^1/_4''$ (6mm) from the diagonal fold.

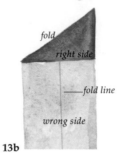

fold

right side

fold line

wrong side

**13b**

Open out lengthwise fold of binding, leaving diagonal fold in place. With right sides together and one raw edge of binding even with raw edge of quilt top, stitch binding to one side of quilt for about 3–4" (7.5–10cm). Do *not* start on a corner.

Break thread and lift presser foot. Fold binding back to doubled position along fold line, then, starting a little way down from diagonal fold line, continue to stitch binding to quilt through all layers, stitching until you are $^1/_4''$ (6mm) away from the first corner. With the needle in the down position, pivot quilt on needle (**Diagram 13c**).

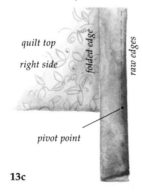

quilt top

right side

folded edge

raw edges

pivot point

**13c**

Stitch a further $^1/_4''$ (6mm) on the diagonal, towards corner of quilt top.

Break thread. Remove quilt from machine, fold binding back onto the stitching line you have just made, then stitch binding to next side of quilt, starting at edge of quilt top (**Diagram 13d**). Complete all corners in this manner as you come to them.

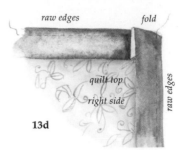

raw edges      fold

quilt top

right side

raw edges

**13d**

When you have stitched the binding to all edges of the quilt and returned to the starting point, leave needle in the down position and place the end of the binding over the single thickness sewn at the start. Cut off any excess length of binding and tuck the end into the pocket formed at the starting point. Continue to stitch through all thicknesses to complete (**Diagram 13e**).

folded edge

fold

raw edges

**13e**

Turn binding to back of quilt and slip-stitch in place over seam, hand-sewing mitres at corners.

**Single** Multiply finished width of binding by 2 and add on $^1/_2''$ (1.2cm) for seam allowance. Referring to **Diagram 13a** and instructions in "Double Binding", cut and join enough fabric strips to go around edges of quilt, plus extra for mitres, seam allowances and ease.

Turn under one long raw edge of binding. Fold down one end of binding on the diagonal, press. Trim edge $^1/_4''$ (6mm) from diagonal fold.

With right sides together and unpressed raw edge of binding even with raw edge of quilt top, stitch binding to one side of quilt. Do *not* start on a corner. Mitre corners, following instructions and **Diagrams 13c** and **13d** in "Straight Binding: Double".

Turn binding to back of quilt and slip-stitch pressed edge in place over seam, hand-sewing mitres at corners.

### Bias Binding

Use bias strips to bind a quilt with scalloped or curved edges.

**Cutting and joining strips** To cut bias strips, fold fabric so that lengthwise and crosswise grains align (the bias is at a 45° angle to the selvedge). Measuring out from the fold line, mark and cut bias strips $1^3/_8''$ (3.5cm) wide, or to desired width (**Diagram 14a**).

Join strips to give desired bias length by stitching across straight grain (**Diagram 14b**).

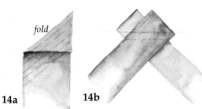

14a    14b

**Cutting continuous strips** If you don't want to join individual strips, you can make a continuous bias strip. Fold a large square of fabric diagonally, and cut along fold line. Place two of the short edges of the resulting triangles together, right sides facing, and stitch (**Diagram 15a**). Press seam allowances open, mark strips of desired width so that they run across seam, marking each strip with a letter (**Diagram 15b**). With right sides together, join ends of parallelogram to form a ring, joining A strip to B strip and so on (**Diagram 15c**). Following the marked lines, cut around the ring in a continuous spiral (**Diagram 15d**).

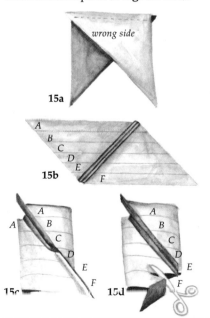

wrong side

15a

15b

15c    15d

**Applying to quilt edges** To bind a curved edge, press bias strip in half lengthwise, wrong sides together, then press under $^1/_4''$ (6mm) along raw edges. Open out binding. Turn under $^1/_4''$ (6mm) at one end of binding. Beginning with turned end, and with right sides together and raw edges even, pin binding to edges of quilt top (**Diagram 16a**). Stitch in place along fold line. Fold binding to quilt back, slip-stitch folded edge into stitching line (**Diagram 16b**).

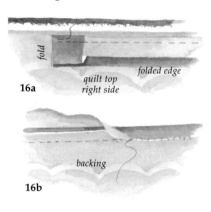

fold

quilt top
right side

folded edge

16a

backing

16b

*Corded Piping*
Fold bias strip, wrong sides together, over piping cord. Using a zipper foot, stitch next to cord (**Diagram 17a**).

Pin piping to edge of fabric piece, with right sides together and aligning raw edges. Using a zipper foot, stitch in place (**Diagram 17b**).

Pin and stitch remaining fabric piece in position (**Diagram 17c**).

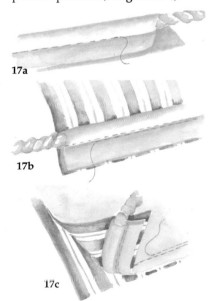

17a

17b

17c

To apply piping around corners, clip from raw edge towards stitching (**Diagram 17d**). Pin piping around corner, easing to fit.

17d

## EMBROIDERY STITCHES

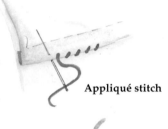

**Appliqué stitch**

**Back-stitch**

**Blanket stitch**

**Stem stitch**

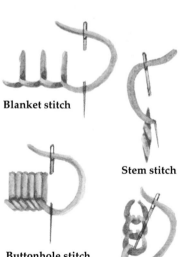

**Buttonhole stitch**

**Chain stitch**

**Bullion stitch**

PROJECT EDITOR: Megan Johnston
PHOTOGRAPHERS: Andrew Elton, Joe Filshie,
Andre Martin, Joss de Groot
STYLISTS: Louise Owens, Georgina Dolling,
Maayke de Ridder
ILLUSTRATOR: Jo McComiskey

HOME LIBRARY STAFF
EDITOR-IN-CHIEF: Mary Coleman
EDITOR: Liz Neate
DESIGNER: Alison Windmill
EDITORIAL COORDINATORS:
Fiona Lambrou, Kate Neil
MANAGING DIRECTOR: Colin Morrison
GROUP PUBLISHER: Paul Dykzeul

PRODUCED BY
The Australian Women's Weekly
Home Library.
COLOUR SEPARATIONS BY
ACP Colour Graphics Pty Ltd, Sydney.
PRINTING BY
Times Printers Pte Limited, Singapore.

PUBLISHED BY
ACP Publishing Pty Limited,
54 Park St, Sydney; GPO Box 4088,
Sydney, NSW 1028.
Ph: (02) 9282 8618  Fax: (02) 9267 9438.
AWWHomeLib@publishing.acp.com.au

AUSTRALIA:
Distributed by Network Distribution
Company, GPO Box 4088, Sydney, NSW 1028.
Ph: (02) 9282 8777  Fax: (02) 9264 3278.
UNITED KINGDOM:
Distributed in the UK by
Australian Consolidated Press (UK),
20 Galowhill Rd, Brackmills, Northampton
NN4 7EE, (01604) 760 456.
CANADA:
Distributed in Canada by Whitecap Books Ltd,
351 Lynn Ave, North Vancouver, BC, V7J 2C4,
(604) 980 9852.
NEW ZEALAND:
Distributed in New Zealand by
Netlink Distribution Company,
17B Hargreaves St, Level 5, College Hill,
Auckland 1, (9) 302 7616.
SOUTH AFRICA:
Distributed in South Africa by Intermag,
PO Box 57394, Springfield 2137 Johannesburg,
SA, (011) 491 7534.

Creative Patchwork, with Appliqué and
Quilting.
ISBN 1 86396 090 2

1. Patchwork – patterns. 2. Appliqué –
patterns. 3. Quilting – patterns.
I. Title: Australian
Women's Weekly. (Series: Australian
Women's Weekly Home Library.)

746.46041

© ACP Publishing Pty Limited 1998
ACN 053 273 546